MEASURE THE POSSIBILITIES

WITH

Omnigrid®

NANCY JOHNSON-SREBRO

Measure The Possibilities with Omnigrid®
©1999 Silver Star, Inc.

Exclusive Distributor

C&T Publishing, Inc.
P.O. Box 1456
Lafayette, CA 94549
(800) 284-1114
Website: www.ctpub.com

Published by:
Silver Star, Inc.
55 Saddle Lake Rd.
Tunkhannock, PA 18657
All Rights Reserved

ISBN 0-9638764-0-6

Printed in China
10 9 8 7 6 5 4

To All Quiltmakers...

You have kindled and built in me a "quilting spirit" that's like a bonfire!
And for that, I will be eternally grateful.

Acknowledgments

Thank you to:

Debbie Grow, Laurie Mace, Marcia Rickansrud and Ethel Whalen for taking countless hours out of their busy schedules to proof-read and sew quilts for this book.

Karen Brown, a non-quilting friend, for her unyielding patience and support.

Jeana Kimball and Pepper Cory for their encouragement.

More members of the "Always In Stitches" quilt group: Maria Carr, Janet McCarroll, Shirley Joyce and Roxanne Sidorek. Your support is greatly appreciated.

James Brogan for giving so freely of his time.

Steve Appel for his expertise in photography, and Chitra Publications for their kind assistance in helping with this project.

Conrad Associates, Clarks Summit, Pennsylvania, for their fantastic computer skills.

Randy and Peggy Schafer, whose dedication to producing quality products has benefited quiltmakers everywhere.

My children Mark, Alan, Karen and my husband, Frank.

Special Thanks

Special thanks to the following companies for providing various quilting supplies. It certainly made my job easier!

Alaska Dyeworks
300 W. Swanson Ave.
Suite 101
Wasilla, AK 99654

Clotilde
(Fine Silk Pins)
B3000
Louisiana, MO 63353

Fasco/Fabric Sales Co., Inc.
(Roberta Horton Fabrics)
6250 Stanley Ave. So.
Seattle, WA 98108

P&B Textiles
(Elly Sienkiewicz Fabrics)
1580 Gilbreth Road
Burlingame, CA 94010

The Stencil Company
(Quilting Stencils)
28 Castlewood Dr.
Cheektowaga, NY 14227

RJR Fashion Fabrics
(Jinny Beyer Fabrics)
13748 S. Gramercy Pl.
Gardena, CA 90249

Mountain Mist®
(Batting)
100 Williams St.
Cincinnati, OH 45215

Fairfield Processing
(Batting)
88 Rose Hill Ave.
Danbury, CT 06810

Warm Products, Inc.
(Batting)
954 E. Union Street
Seattle, WA 98122

TABLE OF CONTENTS

Continued

TABLE OF CONTENTS

Patterns

Maximizing Your Omnigrid® Rulers

Problem Solving Guide For Rotary Cutting

About The Author

Dear Quilting Friends:

I have been rotary cutting since 1984. In this time span I've rotary cut over 1000 miniatures, over 200 quilts and more wallhangings than I can remember. From these many projects my rotary cutter, ruler, mat and sewing machine have become like best friends. After reading this book, you should also come to appreciate your equipment.

In **Measure The Possibilities with Omnigrid**®, you will find the most up-to-date information on rotary cutting. I have developed many new techniques to simplify cutting and increase its accuracy. The opening chapter includes important information on how to properly handle your equipment for less hand fatigue, and why you will always do well to use **Omnigrid**® rulers and an **OMNIMAT**® for your rotary cutting needs.

If you have ever wondered about the grain line on fabric, Chapter 2 will answer all those questions and more. This information is critical to award-winning projects. With my Grain Line Chart©, you will never have to guess how to use grain line to maximum advantage.

This rotary cutting book has over **170** graphics showing **left** and **right** handed quilters how to successfully rotary cut the full range **(23)** of the most used shapes in quiltmaking. Also, you will never have to guess the correct seam allowance to add to these shapes. I have included this information and more. With this knowledge, you will be able to rotary cut literally hundreds of quilt patterns. Also, if you are currently using your rotary cutting equipment only for quiltmaking, you will want to read the section on maximizing **Omnigrid**® rulers. These rulers have become invaluable to artists involved in many different techniques and crafts.

In **Measure The Possibilities with Omnigrid**®, I have chosen several patterns which may be mixed or matched together to create a wallhanging or quilt. I have also taken what I call a "Master Pattern" and have used it in different settings. To gain practical color skills and confidence, I have **not** included a supply list for each pattern. Be adventurous! Try rotary cutting and piecing many different colors of 100% cotton fabrics to make your block. Then sew the blocks together to create a one-of-a-kind quilt. Use the colored photos featured in this book for inspiration. And finally, please send me a colored photo or two of your wallhangings or quilts. I would love to see them.

No book of this scope would be complete without a problem solving guide. I have often thought that an instructional book without a problem solving guide is like a new car that's sold without the owner's manual! So I've included one. In my guide I state the likely problem and how to prevent it; or if the problem has already occurred, how to fix it. One quick glance and you'll have the answer. This is where you can benefit from my experience of rotary cutting over 1000 miniatures.

Now, let's rotary cut and create some gorgeous quilts, and forget about those templates!

Nancy

P.S. *If you are looking for more blocks that don't require templates, my book,* **Timeless Treasures**©*, includes 50 block patterns which are totally rotary cut. I also included many of my sewing and pressing secrets.*

*W*hen my husband helped me update the classes in one of my recent traveling brochures, he thought I should include a class on rotary cutting. I said, "No one will pay me to teach rotary cutting". But he persisted and I decided to give it a try. Little did I know it would become one of my most requested classes!

The year 1988 was a bittersweet one for me. I was suffering with wrist pain and I had to have wrist operations for Carpal Tunnel Syndrome. After taking a few weeks off to recuperate, I was ready to charge ahead with quiltmaking. To my surprise, I had to re-evaluate how I was using my hands and what type of equipment I was using. I had been unknowingly stressing my hands when quiltmaking. I also discovered the two **musts** for successful projects. You **must** have the correct equipment and you **must** know how to properly use that equipment. Through trial and error I have developed methods that have helped thousands overcome rotary cutting problems. In this chapter I will share these ideas and methods with you.

Rotary Cutter

When my friend, Marty, gave me a rotary cutter, ruler, and mat for Christmas, I kept thinking, there is no way this pizza cutter is going to work! I was wrong. A big "Thank You" to the inventor of the rotary cutter, whoever you are.

This piece of equipment has proven to be invaluable. The rotary cutter has almost totally replaced scissors in quiltmaking. The reason for this is accuracy. When you cut with scissors, the fabric is being slightly lifted off the table. Consequently, your cutting will be inaccurate. With a rotary cutter, this will not happen because you are cutting against a perfectly straight edge, the ruler, and you are not lifting the fabric off the mat.

I am constantly asked, "Which is the best rotary cutter to buy?". This is a hard question to answer because everyone's hands are different. I personally use a large yellow Olfa® rotary cutter. Here are some reasons why:

#1 This cutter fits my hand size best. After the operation on my wrists, I discovered I had been holding my cutter improperly. I then had to find the best way to hold the cutter for minimum stress on my hands. You will notice when you stand up, your hands will naturally fall to your side with the back of the hand facing outward. After experimenting, I discovered that by placing the bottom of the rotary cutter in the palm of my hand and my first finger on the etched ridge on the side of the cutter, my hand would still fall naturally to my side **and** the back of my hand was still facing outward. But, if I held the cutter with **all** my fingers wrapped around the handle, the bottom of the cutter was not in the palm of my hand, and my hand did not fall naturally to my side. It was slightly twisted at the wrist.

This forces your wrist to do all the work while cutting. Incidentally, this is the way most people hold their cutter. Another poor way to hold the cutter is with your thumb on top of the cutter and your fingers wrapped around its handle. Your wrist has to work even harder. I've found both methods cause pain in the wrist area.

Try holding your rotary cutter in the three different positions I just described. You will notice how much more comfortable the cutter will feel in the palm of your hand.

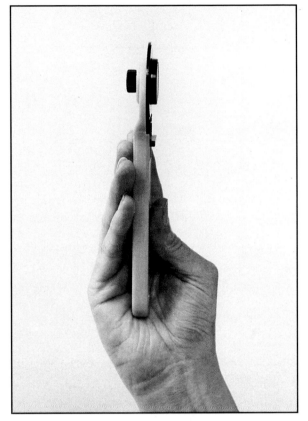

Rotary cutter in the palm of the hand. First finger on the etched ridge.

#2 The etched ridge on the side of the Olfa® cutter is not there for decoration! This surface is designed for placement of your first finger; during classes I refer to this as your "driving" finger. By placing your first finger on the etched ridge, you are now able to "steer" the rotary cutter. How many times have you been cutting and the cutter veers away from the ruler? It happens because you did not have your finger where it should be. Almost all rotary cutters have an etched ridge.

#3 I like the Olfa® cutter because of the manual safety guard. To open, you gently pull down on the black guard. To close, you simply push the black guard up. **You** are in **control** of opening and closing the cutter. If the guard is hard to pull down or push up, slightly loosen the screw on the back of the cutter. Tighten the screw if the guard moves too easily.

#4 The cutter is made for left or right handed people. You don't have to switch the blade from one side of the cutter to the other. Since I cut both left and right handed, I found this to be a plus. Left handers have been generally forgotten by many product manufacturers, but not by Olfa® or **Omnigrid®**.

✳ If your rotary cutter drags through the fabric it may mean one or more of the following:

- You are not holding the cutter at a 45° angle (relative to the cutting mat). This is a common problem. If you hold the cutter at a lesser angle, you will have less effective cutting pressure. Also, the fabric may bind against the back of the cutter.

- Make sure the blade is butted against the ruler. **Do not tilt** the cutter towards the ruler or away from the ruler.

- Your tension is too loose or tight. Loosen or tighten the screw as appropriate.

- The blade is dull. Change the blade.

- You need to put more pressure on the cutter when cutting.

- You are trying to cut through too many layers of fabric.

✳ Take the cutter apart periodically for cleaning. Also, place a small drop of sewing machine oil on the blade. This will help the blade turn more freely. Cleaning and oiling your cutter are two of those little secrets that contribute to precision cutting.

✳ Always keep a sharp blade in the cutter. A dull blade causes inaccurate cutting and unnecessary hand fatigue.

✳ Always close the cutter the second you are done cutting. The blade is very sharp. If you accidentally drop the opened cutter, the blade will be nicked, not to mention what would happen if it fell on your foot.

✳ A symptom of a nicked blade is when you are cutting and you miss a thread...a thread...a thread. Replace the blade immediately. Pay attention when disassembling the cutter, so you can put it back together properly.

✳ After prewashing and drying your fabric, you will find it much easier to rotary cut and sew if you press it using Magic® Sizing. This spray sizing (not starch) puts the body back into the fabric.

✳ Do not use the rotary cutter on surfaces not designed for it. I have seen students try to use wood, plastic, glass, and linoleum for their cutting mat. It will cause the blade to dull very quickly.

✳ Save the old blades for cutting your child's school pictures apart, card board, wallpaper, etc. They work wonderfully.

*A*fter reading this chapter, I suspect you will run out and buy an **Omnigrid®** ruler if you don't already own one. After making over 1000 miniature quilts without templates (some pieces are as small as 1/4"), I can say with confidence that **Omnigrid®**'s rulers are simply the best. Here are some reasons why I feel this way:

#1 Right from the start, **Omnigrid®** manufactured their rulers for both left and right handed people. The top and bottom of the ruler are marked with two sets of numbers - one for left handed people and one for right handed people. I cannot tell you how many times I've been told by students how happy they are that **Omnigrid®** rulers are designed for use by everyone.

My quilting partner, Debbie Grow, is left handed; though when I lecture, I call her my "Right Hand!" She knows, and constantly tells me, how hard it is for left handed people to find a product that works for them. To become a better teacher, I also taught myself to cut left handed. It is easier than you think. So I have personal knowledge of the left handers' dilemma as well.

#2 Why would you want a ruler with only black lines when you are working with dark fabrics? It's difficult to see the markings on the dark fabric. This is why **Omnigrid®** makes their rulers with contrasting colors - black lines and yellow lines. The **black line** is the actual measuring line. The yellow lines are wider and are there just to highlight the black. I tell students, when the edge of the fabric is totally hidden under the desired marking (i.e. 2 1/2" marking) you are correct. Consequently, you don't want to have your fabric to the left of the yellow line or to the right of the yellow line. If you do, your cutting will be either smaller or larger than desired.

#3 **Omnigrid®** rulers have all the markings you will ever need to successfully measure once, and cut once, with confidence. Eleven of the rulers have markings in 1/8" increments and two of the rulers have an added bonus of 1/16" increments. (Great for miniature work).

#4 These rulers are laser cut and printed to within .002 inch accuracy. Unlike other rulers I've tried, the printing is accurate. This accuracy is increased by printing on the underside of the ruler. This eliminates the distortion which is created when you look through the ruler to the fabric.

#5 The markings have not worn off any of my rulers, which are heavily used. Of course, you must take care of the ruler. All rulers will scratch if you throw them around. I am careful not to place the ruler on top of rotary cutters, ink pens, paper clips, etc. If you accidentally get glue or ink on the ruler, simply clean the glue spots, etc. with rubbing alcohol. Do **not** use nail polish remover. It will remove the markings on the ruler.

#6 Angles, angles, and more angles. This ruler has it all! I tell students that once you master cutting straight strips, squares and rectangles, the next challenge is angles. There are left and right 30°, 45°, and 60° markings on the lower part of the ruler. By having the angle markings there, it allows you to work closer to your body instead of leaning over your work.

*W*hen I started quiltmaking in 1984, I used a solid green mat that had little bumps on it. It seemed okay at the time, but I was never really satisfied with it. I started experimenting with alternatives. After a few years of testing, I found there are a lot of differences in mats. Here are a few:

#1 The green mat with the little bumps started to shed green flakes after I used it a bit. I guess I had worn it out.

#2 The white and frosted looking mats seemed to dull my blades very quickly. I found I was cutting deeper into these mats than the green mats. Also, the mat did not seem to heal properly.

#3 Some but not all mats are reversible to the same color. Don't buy a mat that isn't reversible to a contrasting color, i.e. light-dark. A reversible mat is like getting two mats for the price of one.

#4 Some of the grid markings on the mats are not accurate. When buying a mat, take along your **Omnigrid**® ruler to see if the markings on the mat line up with the markings on the ruler.

#5 Some mats have a slight odor to them.

OMNIMAT®

Now that you have my comments on mats, I will tell you why I like the **OMNIMAT**®. After I threw away my green mat with the bumps, I bought a smooth green mat. It was dark green on both sides. I couldn't believe how much longer the blade in my rotary cutter stayed sharp. I used this mat until the **OMNIMAT**® was introduced. Since I make my living as a quilt teacher, I feel it is important to try all the new products on the market. (At least that's what I tell my husband!) So, of course, I bought an **OMNIMAT**®. Here are the reasons why I like it:

#1 The primary reason is that the mat reverses from a medium green to a light gray. Since I had to start wearing glasses for close up work, the bi-colored mat was like a gift of sight. By flipping the mat to the side that creates the greatest contrast between your fabric and the mat, I found I had less eye strain.

#2 The grid markings are accurate with the **Omnigrid**® ruler.

#3 The mat is smooth, so my rotary cutter blades stay sharp longer.

#4 The mats have no odor. This may be a small thing to some of you, but I always wonder what exotic chemical I'm breathing.

#5 The mats come in six different sizes. You can find any size you need. They even make a mat that is 48" x 96". Now that's big quiltmaking!

#6 You can safely clean the **OMNIMAT**®. If you happen to get a pencil mark, etc. on the mat, clean with a tiny amount of diluted dishwashing liquid or Soft Scrub® on a soft cloth. Rub lightly. Rinse with clean water.

𝒰p until a few years ago, I only vaguely knew about the grain of fabric. Since I've always rotary cut strips of fabric crosswise grain, then recut the strips into the desired shape, my piecing had always turned out fine. When I started teaching quilt-making, I had a student ask me how I knew I was cutting "on the true grain". It was time for me to do some research!

I learned that when fabric is being woven in the factory, three types of grain are created.

• **Lengthwise Grain:** This grain description means the threads run the length of the fabric. There is almost no stretch to the fabric on the lengthwise grain.

• **Crosswise Grain:** This grain line describes threads that run with the width of the fabric. As you probably know, the width of most fabric is 44". There is slight stretch to the fabric on the crosswise grain.

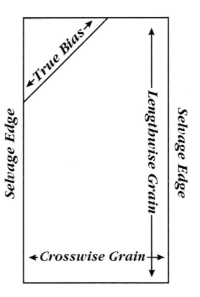

• **Bias Grain:** This grain line is formed when the fabric is cut on the diagonal. A true bias is when the fabric is cut at a 45° angle. Fabric cut at any other angle (not 45°) is untrue bias. The truc bias has the most stretch of all.

• **Straight Grain:** This term may refer to either lengthwise grain or crosswise grain. I'm including it so you may compare it with the bias grain description.

Working with fabric for many years, I have found that few fabrics are woven so the grain lines (threads) appear straight across the fabric. I'm sure this is due to the different processes involved in manufacturing fabric. I try to cut my strips as close to the straight grain (lengthwise/crosswise) as I can.

I included my Grain Line Chart© to help you see where the grain lines are on the shapes featured in **Measure The Possibilities with Omnigrid®**. This chart will also be invaluable when drafting patterns from other sources.

NOTE: To minimize any stretching of the fabric, try at all times to keep the Straight Grain (not bias) on the outside edges of the block or quilt.

𝒯his Grain Line Chart© is based upon cutting strips of fabric on the **crosswise grain,** and then cutting into the desired shape.

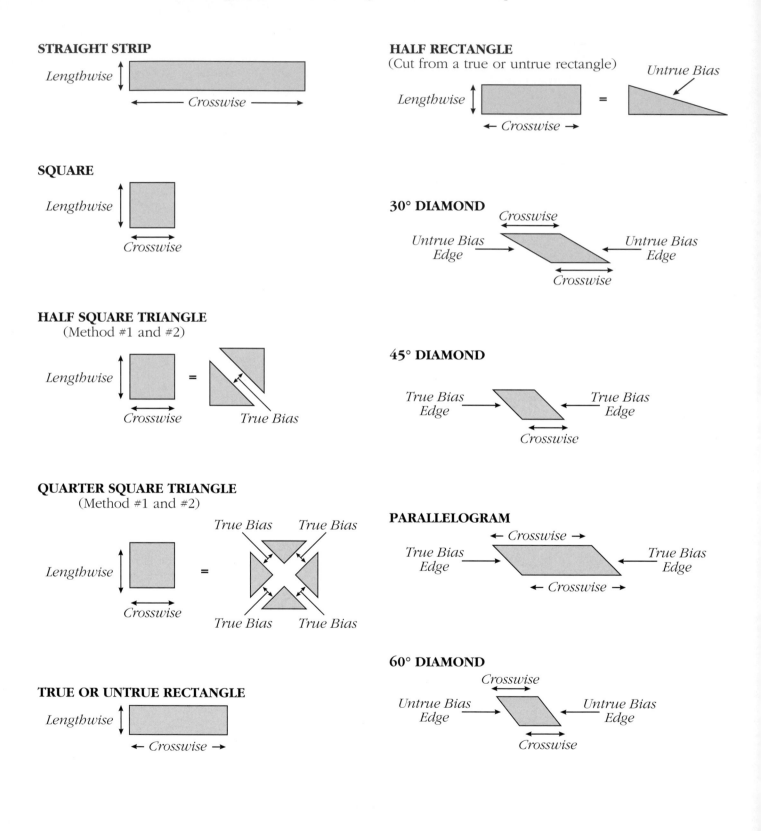

STRAIGHT STRIP

Lengthwise
Crosswise

HALF RECTANGLE
(Cut from a true or untrue rectangle)

Lengthwise
Crosswise
=
Untrue Bias

SQUARE

Lengthwise
Crosswise

30° DIAMOND

Crosswise
Untrue Bias Edge
Untrue Bias Edge
Crosswise

HALF SQUARE TRIANGLE
(Method #1 and #2)

Lengthwise
Crosswise
=
True Bias

45° DIAMOND

True Bias Edge
True Bias Edge
Crosswise

QUARTER SQUARE TRIANGLE
(Method #1 and #2)

Lengthwise
Crosswise
=
True Bias True Bias
True Bias True Bias

PARALLELOGRAM

Crosswise
True Bias Edge
True Bias Edge
Crosswise

TRUE OR UNTRUE RECTANGLE

Lengthwise
Crosswise

60° DIAMOND

Crosswise
Untrue Bias Edge
Untrue Bias Edge
Crosswise

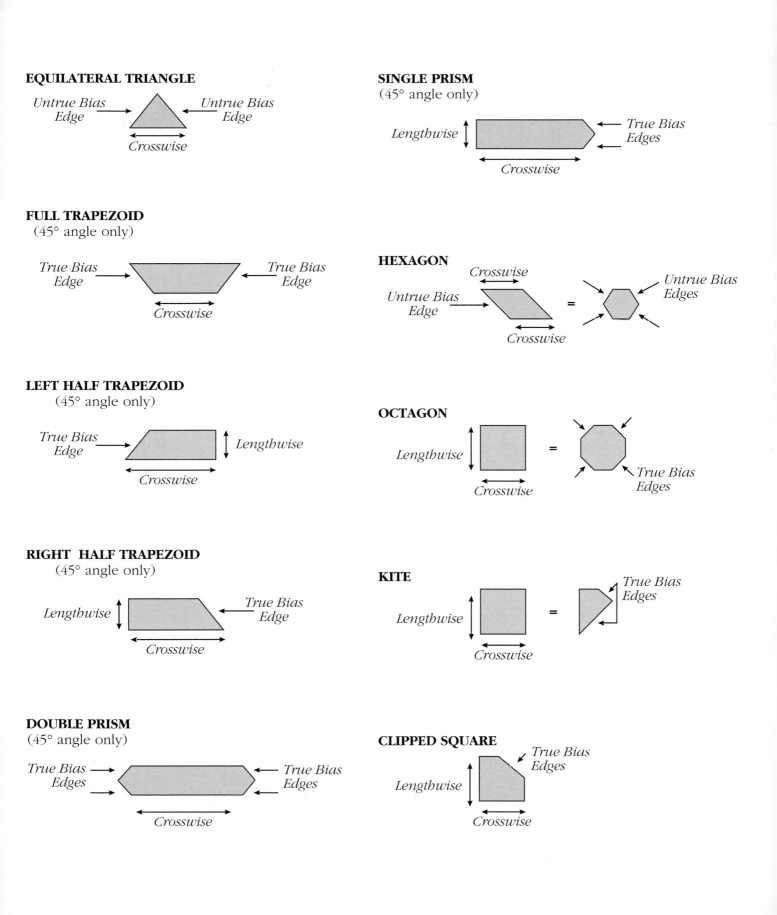

EQUILATERAL TRIANGLE

Untrue Bias Edge → ← Untrue Bias Edge

Crosswise

FULL TRAPEZOID
(45° angle only)

True Bias Edge → ← True Bias Edge

Crosswise

LEFT HALF TRAPEZOID
(45° angle only)

True Bias Edge →

Lengthwise

Crosswise

RIGHT HALF TRAPEZOID
(45° angle only)

Lengthwise

True Bias Edge ←

Crosswise

DOUBLE PRISM
(45° angle only)

True Bias Edges →

True Bias Edges ←

Crosswise

SINGLE PRISM
(45° angle only)

Lengthwise ↕

True Bias Edges ←

Crosswise

HEXAGON

Crosswise

Untrue Bias Edge →

Crosswise

= Untrue Bias Edges

OCTAGON

Lengthwise ↕

Crosswise

= True Bias Edges

KITE

Lengthwise ↕

Crosswise

= True Bias Edges

CLIPPED SQUARE

True Bias Edges

Lengthwise ↕

Crosswise

To practice cutting a straight edge on your fabric, you will need a 6" x 24" ruler, a 17" x 23" mat, and a one yard (36" x44") piece of fabric.

STEP ONE: Fold the fabric once, selvage to selvage. The top edge of the folded fabric will not be even - due to washing, drying, and the way it was cut at the store. Also, make sure there are no wrinkles of fabric along the fold. The fabric will now measure approximately 22" in width and 36" in length. Place the fabric on the mat with the fold at the top, farthest away from you. The selvages will be at the bottom, nearest to you.

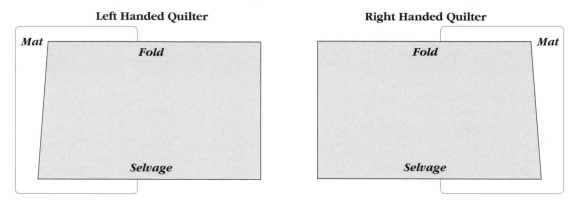

STEP TWO: Place the ruler's short side (6") along the fold. Do this as accurately as you can. The long (24") side of the ruler will be parallel with the left hand edge of the mat for left handed quilters, and parallel with the right hand edge of the mat for right handed quilters.

Firmly place the thumb of your (left) right hand on the bottom of the ruler and your four finger tips 6" - 7" up the ruler. Holding the rotary cutter as described on page 6 and 7, start cutting **away** from you until you are even with your finger tips.

Don't lift the rotary cutter! While keeping the rotary cutter stationary, carefully move your thumb up to your fingers. Next, press down with your thumb and move your four fingers up the ruler approximately 6". I call this "hand walking". Continue cutting until you are again even with your finger tips. Stop cutting. Keep the rotary blade in the fabric. Move your thumb up to your fingers. Press down with your thumb. Move your four fingers up the ruler approximately another 6". Rotary cut. Continue the "hand walking" method until your entire strip is completely cut. You have now "squared up" the fabric.

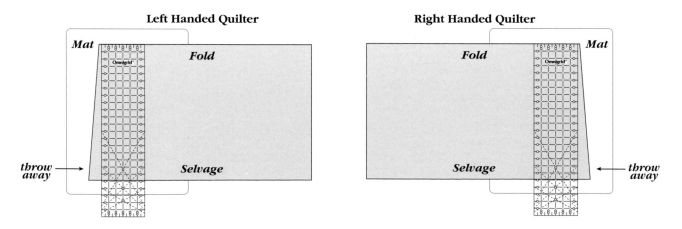

NOTE: *The ruler will never slip if you use the hand walking method. Remember you only want to rotary cut the fabric that is being stabilized by your finger tips on the ruler.*

*I*n rotary cutting almost any shape, you will first start out with a straight strip of fabric, then recut the strip into the desired shape. In this exercise I will show you how I cut straight strips. I always use a 6" x 24" **Omnigrid**® ruler and a 17" x 23" **OMNIMAT**®.

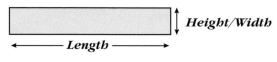

Add on seam allowance to the <u>FINISHED</u> size of a Straight Strip:

> **Add ¹/₂" to the height/width** (The words height and width are interchangeable)
> **Add ¹/₂" to the length**

Example: Desired finished strip size: 2 ¹/₂" x 43 ¹/₂"

Size of strip to cut: 3" x 44"
> 2 ¹/₂" + ¹/₂" = 3"
> 43 ¹/₂" + ¹/₂" = 44"

STEP ONE: Follow Steps One and Two on page 14 for cutting a straight edge.

STEP TWO: After cutting a straight edge on the fabric, turn the mat 180°, one half of a full turn. Do not lift the fabric off the mat. If you lift the fabric off the mat, you will disturb the freshly cut straight edge. Now the fold is closest to your body. Position the long side of the ruler over the straight edge that you have just cut. Move the ruler until the straight edge of the fabric lines up with the 3" marking, and the bottom of the ruler is even with the fold. Use the hand walking method to rotary cut a 3" x 44" strip.

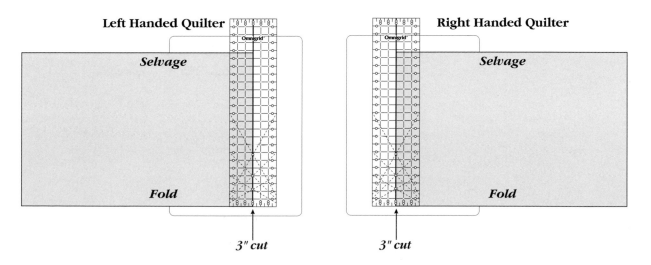

Read the next section on "How To Avoid The Dreaded "V" Cut" before you continue cutting more straight strips.

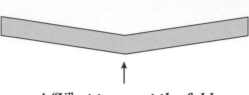

A "V" appears at the fold

$\mathcal{W}$hen I first began rotary cutting, I was not consistently getting nice straight strips. I thought that after I made my first straight cut, I was ready to rotary cut for hours! But after only a few minutes of cutting, I realized my straight strips were no longer straight. They had developed a slight "V" at the fold. See the exaggerated illustration above.

Through a lot of trial and error, I realized there are at least two reasons why you get "V" cuts; and I also figured out how you can avoid these problems.

PROBLEM #1: Referring to page 14, Step Two, you placed the ruler's short side (6") along the fold. Therefore you are "In Square" with the fold for only 6", the width of the ruler. After cutting 6" worth of strips, you are starting to get "out of square".

HOW TO AVOID THIS PROBLEM: After cutting 6" worth of strips, you must "resquare" the fabric with the new fold. This is extremely important to maintain cutting accuracy. After "resquaring", continue cutting straight strips until you have cut 6" worth of straight strips, then you must "resquare" again. Repeat this procedure every 6".

PROBLEM #2: If you look back at Step One on page 14, you will notice I have only folded the fabric once before I began rotary cutting. Some folks like to fold their fabric one more time. Thus they will be cutting through four layers of fabric instead of two. This in itself is not a problem.

HOW TO AVOID THIS PROBLEM: The problem arises when the student doesn't realize that she/he now has a choice of which fold to "square up" with. Whichever fold you choose to "square up" with, you must work from that same fold at all times. You cannot "square up" with one fold and then work from the other fold.

When I am at home working on my quilts, I never fold the fabric more than once, so I only cut through two layers at a time. Remember the more layers of fabric you rotary cut through, the more inaccurate your cutting becomes. To prove this, stack 6 to 8 layers of fabric together. Now place the ruler as if you were going to cut a 2" strip. You will notice that the ruler acts like a teeter totter. The bottom layers of fabric will shift slightly which will cause you to cut inaccurately.

Now that you understand how to avoid the dreaded "V" cut, practice cutting and "resquaring" the following straight strips to be used in the upcoming rotary cutting section: 3 - 3" x 44" strips, 1 - 3 $^1/_8$" x 22" strip, and 1 - 5" x 44" strip.

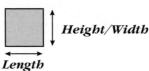

Height/Width

Length

$\mathcal{O}$nce you master cutting straight strips, it is simple to recut the strips into squares, rectangles, diamonds, etc. I have found it is easier to use a 6" x 12", 3" x 18" or 6" square to recut the strips into smaller shapes. A 6" x 12" **Omnigrid**® ruler will be used in rest of the diagrams.

Add on seam allowance to the <u>FINISHED</u> size of a Square:

> **Add 1/2" to the height/width** (The words height and width
>   are interchangeable)
> **Add 1/2" to the length**

Example: Desired finished square: 2 1/2"

Size of square to cut: 3"
    2 1/2" + 1/2" = 3"

STEP ONE: Place one of the 3" x 22" strips on the mat. (The strip is really 44" long, but is folded in half to equal 22". You will be cutting through two layers at a time). Place the short side (6") of the ruler along the top of the strip. "Square Up" the short side of the strip by cutting off approximately 1/4" from the selvage.

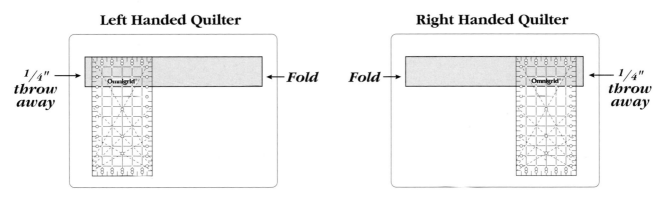

STEP TWO: After cutting the selvage off, turn the mat 180°, half of a turn. Place the ruler on top of the fabric so the 3" marking lines up perfectly with the newly cut edge. Make sure the top of the ruler is even with the top of the strip. Rotary cut.

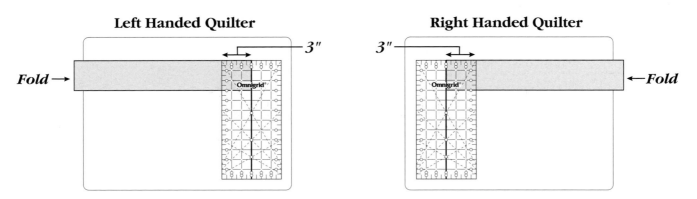

NOTE: *After cutting three 3" squares, "resquare" the edge of the strip as shown in Step One. Follow Step Two to continue cutting squares. Never take a chance by cutting the whole strip into squares without "resquaring" frequently.*

$\mathscr{A}$ half square triangle is simply a square cut in half diagonally, once. It is one of the most widely used shapes in quiltmaking. I will share two different methods with you for cutting this shape.

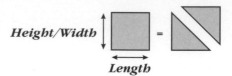

Height/Width

Length

METHOD #1

Add on seam allowance to the <u>FINISHED</u> size of a Square from which two Half Square Triangles will be cut:

Add 7/8" to the height/width (The words height and width are interchangeable)
Add 7/8" to the length

Example: Desired finished square: 2 1/8"

Size of square to cut: 3"
   2 1/8" + 7/8" = 3"

STEP ONE: Place one of the previously cut 3" squares on the mat. Now place the ruler diagonally over the square. Make absolutely sure that the ruler crosses the opposite corners perfectly. Rotary cut. You will have two triangles.

Left Handed Quilter

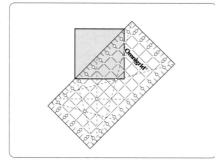

Right Handed Quilter

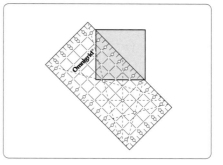

After sewing the two triangles together along the long bias edge and pressing, you will notice the two triangles have what quilters call "dog ears" at the opposite 45° ends. Often times the pressed squares seem elongated, not true squares. To prevent the square from becoming elongated after sewing, you should always cut the dog ears off first. Then press.

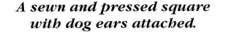

A sewn and pressed square with dog ears attached.

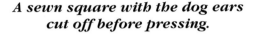

A sewn square with the dog ears cut off before pressing.

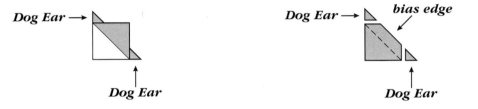

NOTE: *Many times while cutting a square in half diagonally, the square would slip at the last 1/2" of cutting and I would not have a true diagonal (45°) cut. I have had countless students tell me the same thing. After experimenting, I finally discovered that I was not stabilizing the square under the ruler. Now I always place my first finger tip on top of the ruler, directly over the fabric triangle. This way the square cannot move, because of the pressure on the ruler from my finger tip.*

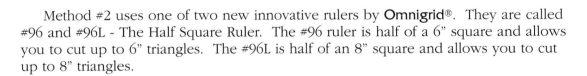

#96 & #96L

METHOD #2

Method #2 uses one of two new innovative rulers by **Omnigrid**®. They are called #96 and #96L - The Half Square Ruler. The #96 ruler is half of a 6" square and allows you to cut up to 6" triangles. The #96L is half of an 8" square and allows you to cut up to 8" triangles.

What is so wonderful about these rulers is that the guesswork has been taken out of cutting a half square triangle because the seam allowances are "built into" the rulers.

Add on seam allowance to the <u>FINISHED</u> size of a Square from which two Half Square Triangles will be cut:

Add ¹/₂" to the height/width (The words height and width
are interchangeable)

NOTE: *Another way of determining the height/width of the strip is to simply measure from the dashed line near the top of the ruler to the bottom line of the desired size.*

Continued

Example: Desired finished square: 2 ¹/₂"

Size of the strip to cut: 3"
    2 ¹/₂" + ¹/₂" = 3"

STEP ONE: Place one of the 3" strips on the mat. "Square Up" the short edge of the strip. Next, position the ruler on the strip with the dashed tip of the ruler over the top edge and the 2 ¹/₂" marking along the bottom of the strip. Rotary cut. Now, rotate the ruler 180°. Line up the 2 ¹/₂" marking along the top of the strip and the dashed line will be along the bottom of the strip. The diagonal edge of the ruler will line up with the freshly cut diagonal edge of the fabric. Rotary cut again. Continue rotating the ruler every other time to cut more triangles. Don't forget to occasionally "resquare" the short end of the strip.

Left Handed Quilter   Right Handed Quilter

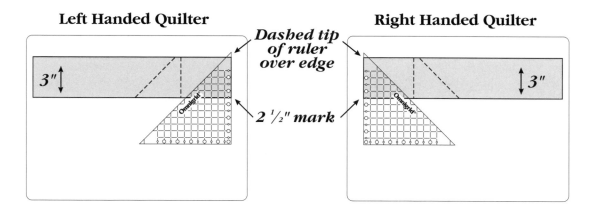

You will notice that this triangle has only one "dog ear" at one end of the triangle.

Dog Ear

NOTE: *A great time saver when using Method #1 or Method #2 is to cut two strips of fabric (a light strip and a dark strip of the desired colors) and place them right sides together making sure all edges align perfectly. (Have the wrong side of the light fabric facing you. It will be easier on your eyes when rotary cutting). Position the ruler according to the method you are using and start cutting. No additional handling is needed when you are ready to sew the triangles together. They are already matched!*

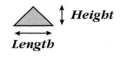

METHOD #1

A quarter square triangle is a square that has been cut in half diagonally, twice. After cutting twice, you will have four identical triangles with the straight grain on the long outside edge of the triangles and the bias on the short inside edges. There are two different methods I will share with you for cutting this shape.

Add on seam allowance to the <u>FINISHED</u> size of the long side of a Quarter Square Triangle:

Add 1 1/4" to the height of a square
Add 1 1/4" to the length of a square

Example: Desired finished length of the long side of a quarter square
triangle: 3 3/4"

Size of square to cut: 5"
3 3/4" + 1 1/4" = 5"

STEP ONE: Cut a 5" square. Place the ruler diagonally over the square. Make absolutely sure that the ruler crosses the opposite corners perfectly. Remember to keep your first finger tip on top of the ruler, directly over the fabric to prevent the square from moving. Rotary cut. You will now have two triangles. Do not separate the two triangles.

Left Handed Quilter   **Right Handed Quilter**

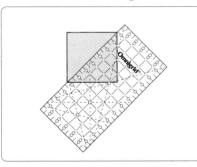   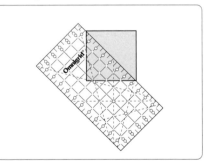

STEP TWO: For the second cut, you will cut the square in half from the opposite corners.

Left Handed Quilter   **Right Handed Quilter**

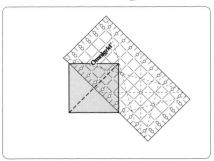   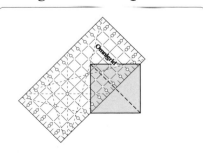

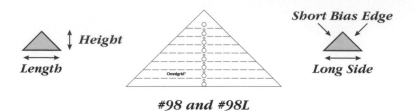

#98 and #98L

METHOD #2

$\mathcal{T}$o help simplify quilter's lives, **Omnigrid**® invented the #98 and #98L - Quarter Square Ruler. The #98 ruler allows you to cut any size quarter square triangle up to 8" on the long side. The #98L allows you to cut any size quarter square triangle up to 12" on the long side.

When using the #98 or #98L, you first cut strips of fabric, then recut the strips into quarter square triangles. Compare this with Method #1, whereby you cut squares, then recut the squares in half diagonally, twice. I always use this ruler when I need one or two quarter square triangles. If I were to use Method #1, I would waste the remaining two or three triangles that were cut. There are also times when I want the design of striped or plaid fabric to lay a certain way in my miniatures and quilts. If I use Method #1, I will get a random pattern in the design, but if I cut strips along the plaid or stripe, I am able to create a consistent design.

For example, a triangle that is cut at the 5" mark will finish to be 5" on the long side (not on the two short bias sides). If you were to measure along the 5" line on the ruler, you would find that it measures 6 1/4". Remember in Method #1, I stated that you must add 1 1/4" to the finished size of the long side of the triangle? Well, you can easily see that 5" + 1 1/4" = 6 1/4". No more guess work! **Omnigrid**® has already designed the 1 1/4" add on seam allowance into the ruler.

Add on seam allowance for the height of a Quarter Square Triangle:

> **Measure from the top of the ruler down to the desired finished length of the long side of the quarter square triangle.**

Example: Desired finished length of the long side: 5"

Height of strip to cut: Measure from the top of the ruler to the 5" line. The height of the strip will be: 3 1/8".

STEP ONE:

Place the 3 1/8" strip on the mat. Place the ruler on the strip so the 5" marking is along the bottom of the strip. The top of the ruler should be touching the top of the strip. Rotary cut. Now rotate the ruler 180° and place the 5" marking along the top of the strip. Rotary cut. Continue rotating the ruler and cutting this way for maximum use of the strip.

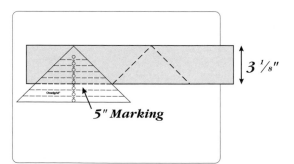

5" Marking

3 1/8"

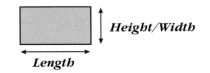

Height/Width

Length

$\mathcal{A}$ true rectangle is a rectangle that is twice as long as high, or vice versa. 2" x 4" or 3" x 6" are examples of true rectangles. An untrue rectangle can be any size. For example, a lattice strip that is 3 ¹/₂" x 9" is an untrue rectangle.

Add on seam allowance to the <u>FINISHED</u> size of a True or Untrue Rectangle:

> **Add ¹/₂" to the height/width** (The words height and width
>   are interchangeable)
> **Add ¹/₂" to the length**

Example: Desired finished size: 2 ¹/₂" x 5" rectangle

Size of rectangle to cut: 3 " x 5 ¹/₂"
    2 ¹/₂" + ¹/₂" = 3"
    5" + ¹/₂" = 5 ¹/₂"

STEP ONE: Place a 3" strip on the mat. "Square Up" the short edge of the strip. Next, place the ruler on top of the strip so the 5 ¹/₂" mark lines up perfectly with the newly cut edge. Make sure the top of the ruler is even with the top of the strip. Rotary cut. For added accuracy, you should always resquare the short end of the strip after cutting three rectangles.

Left Handed Quilter **Right Handed Quilter**

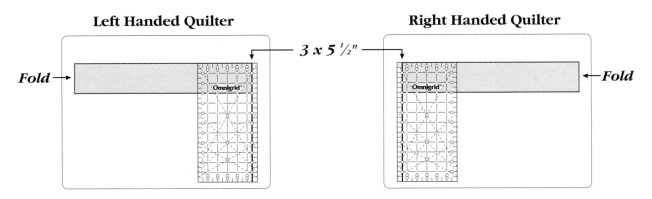

Fold →   — 3 x 5 ¹/₂" —   ←Fold

(from a True Rectangle)

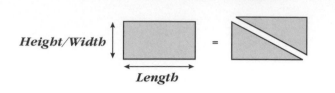

$\mathscr{S}$ome patterns call for a half rectangle. You can easily cut a true or untrue rectangle in half diagonally.

Add on seam allowance to the <u>FINISHED</u> size of a True Rectangle:

Add 11/16" to the height/width (The words height/width
are interchangeable. 11/16" is located between 5/8" and 3/4")

Add 1 5/16" to the length
(1 5/16" is located between 1 1/4" and 1 3/8")

Example: Desired finished true rectangle from which two half rectangles will be cut: 2" x 4" rectangle

Size of rectangle to cut: 2 11/16" x 5 5/16"
2" + 11/16" = 2 11/16"
4" + 1 5/16" = 5 5/16"

STEP ONE: From one of the 3" strips cut a 2 11/16" x 5 5/16" rectangle. (2 11/16" is located between 2 5/8" and 2 3/4". 5 5/16" is located between 5 1/4" and 5 3/8"). Now place the ruler diagonally over the rectangle. Make absolutely sure that the ruler crosses the opposite corners perfectly. Rotary cut. You will have two half rectangles.

Left Handed Quilter   **Right Handed Quilter**

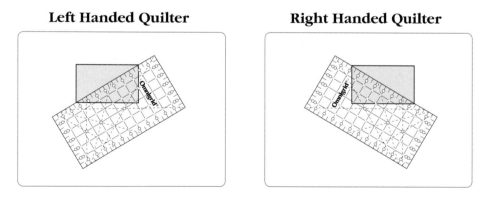

Be aware that you now have two identical half rectangles. To make mirror images of this shape, place two rectangles together, with the wrong sides facing each other. Then rotary cut as shown in Step One.

NOTE: *To determine the add on seam allowance for an Untrue Half Rectangle, draw the finished size rectangle on paper. Draw a diagonal line from corner to corner. Then draw 1/4" seam allowances around the half rectangle. This will be the cutting measurement for the unfinished size of an untrue half rectangle. Rotary cut as shown in Step One.*

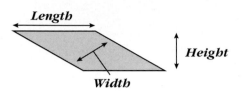

Length

Height

Width

$\mathcal{C}$utting a 30° diamond is easy when using an **Omnigrid**® ruler. All you need to do is add on the **same** amount of seam allowance both to the height and the width. The height and width of a 30° diamond **MUST** be the same. You do not add a seam allowance to the length. The length will automatically be correct after cutting.

Add on seam allowance to the <u>FINISHED</u> size of a 30° Diamond:

Add 1/2" to the height
Add 1/2" to the width

Example: Desired finished size: 2 1/2" - 30° diamond

Height of strip to cut: 3"
2 1/2" + 1/2" = 3"

STEP ONE: Place one of the 3" strips on the mat. Left handed quilters will use the 30° line starting from the lower left edge of the ruler. Right handed quilters will use the 30° line starting from the lower right edge. While placing the ruler on the strip, make sure the 30° line lines up with the bottom of the strip. Rotary cut.

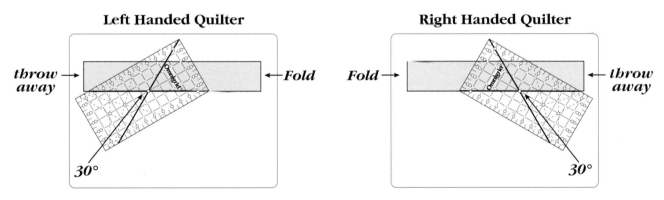

Left Handed Quilter **Right Handed Quilter**

throw away → Fold Fold → throw away

30° 30°

STEP TWO: Turn the mat 180°, half a turn. Find the 3" marking on the top of the ruler. Place the ruler diagonally on the strip so the 3" line is on the freshly cut 30° edge. Also make sure the 30° line is on the bottom of the strip. Rotary cut. If you fold the diamond in half, long point to long point, everything will match.

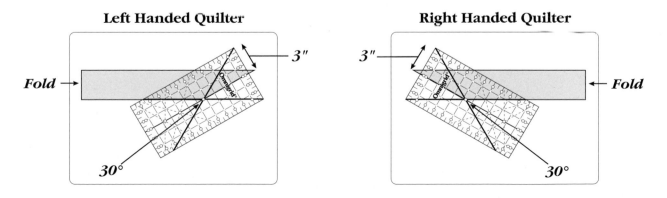

Left Handed Quilter **Right Handed Quilter**

3" 3"

Fold → ← Fold

30° 30°

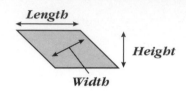

The 45° diamond is the most widely used of all diamonds. Eight Pointed Stars, Lone Stars and hundreds of other star patterns are based on the 45° diamond. All you need to do is add on the **same** amount of seam allowance to both the height and the width. The height and width of a 45° diamond **MUST** be the same. You do not add a seam allowance to the length. The length will automatically be correct after cutting.

Add on seam allowance to the <u>FINISHED</u> size of a 45° Diamond:

Add 1/2" to the height
Add 1/2" to the width

Example: Desired finished size: 2 1/2" - 45° diamond

Height of strip to cut: 3"
2 1/2" + 1/2" = 3"

STEP ONE: Place one of the 3" strips on the mat. Left handed quilters will use the 45° line starting from the lower left edge of the ruler. Right handed quilters will use the 45° line starting from the lower right edge of the ruler. While placing the ruler on the strip, make sure the 45° line lines up with the bottom of the strip. Rotary cut.

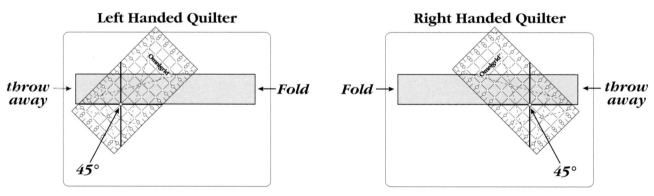

STEP TWO: Turn the mat 180°, half a turn. Find the 3" marking on the top of the ruler. Place the ruler diagonally on the strip so the 3" line is on the freshly cut 45° edge. Also make sure the 45° line is on the bottom of the strip. Rotary cut. If you fold the diamond in half, long point to long point, everything will match.

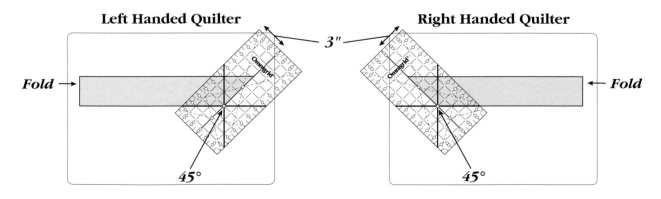

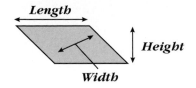

$\mathcal{C}$utting a parallelogram is very much like cutting a 45° diamond. The only difference is that the width of the diagonal cut will **NOT** be the same as the height of the strip. Remember, when cutting a 45° diamond, I stated that the height and the width **MUST** be the same? This is not true when working with a parallelogram.

When cutting a parallelogram you **MUST** include an add on seam allowance to its **height** and **length**. After you add these seam allowances to the finished size of the parallelogram, you can then determine the width of the diagonal cut.

Add on seam allowance to the <u>FINISHED</u> size of a Parallelogram:

Add 1/2" to the height
Add 3/4" to the length

Example: Desired finished size: 2 1/2" x 6 3/8" parallelogram

Height of strip to cut: 3"
    2 1/2" + 1/2" = 3"

STEP ONE: Place one of the 3" strips on the mat. Rotary cut a 45° edge as shown in Step One on page 26. Turn the mat 180°, half of a turn.

STEP TWO: Measure across the top of the strip 7 1/8" and place a small pencil mark there. (6 3/8" is the desired finished length + 3/4" for the add on seam allowance = 7 1/8").

Left Handed Quilter   Right Handed Quilter

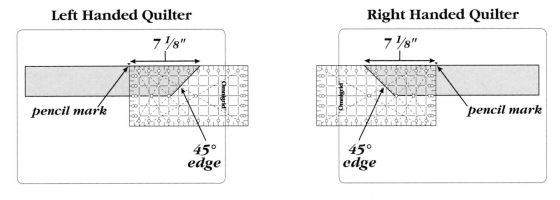

Continued

STEP THREE: To determine the width of the diagonal cut, first place the ruler **diagonally** on the strip so the 45° mark is on the bottom of the strip and the (left) right edge of the ruler lines up with the pencil mark.

The number on the ruler that lines up with the freshly cut 45° edge, is the width of the diagonal cuts. You will see that the ruler lines up with the 5" marking. Consequently, 5" would be the correct cutting measurement for this example.

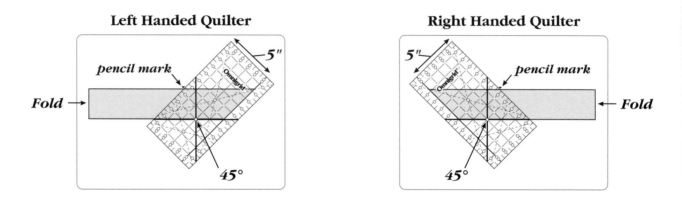

If you were to fold the parallelogram in half, long point to long point, it would not match. If it does match, you have cut a 45° diamond, not a parallelogram.

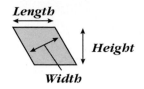

Length

Height

Width

*O*nce you learn how to use the 45° angle on your ruler, the 60° angle will be very easy for you to use. All you need to do is add the **same** amount of seam allowance to both the height and the width. The height and width of a 60° diamond **MUST** be the same. You do not add a seam allowance to the length. The length will automatically be correct after cutting.

Add on seam allowance to the <u>FINISHED</u> size of a 60° Diamond:

Add 1/2" to the height
Add 1/2" to the width

Example: Desired finished size: 2 1/2" - 60° diamond

Height of strip to cut: 3"
2 1/2" + 1/2" = 3"

STEP ONE: Place one of the 3" strips on the mat. Left handed quilters will use the 60° line starting from the lower left edge of the ruler. Right handed quilters will use the 60° line starting from the lower right edge of the ruler. While placing the ruler on the strip, make sure the 60° line lines up with the bottom of the strip. Rotary cut.

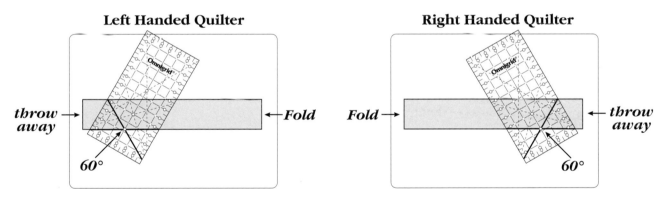

Left Handed Quilter   **Right Handed Quilter**

throw away → ← Fold   Fold → ← throw away

60°   60°

STEP TWO: Turn the mat 180°, half a turn. Find the 3" marking on the top of the ruler. Place the ruler diagonally on the strip so the 3" line is on the freshly cut 60° edge. Also make sure the 60° line is on the bottom of the strip. Rotary cut. If you fold the diamond in half, long point to long point, everything will match.

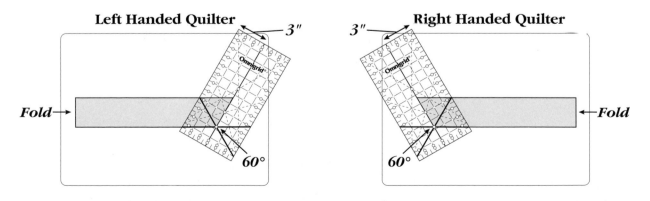

Left Handed Quilter   **Right Handed Quilter**

3"   3"

Fold →   ← Fold

60°   60°

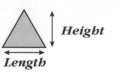

Height

Length

 $\mathscr{A}$n equilateral triangle is a triangle with all three sides of equal length. The well known Thousand Pyramid pattern uses this shape. This is a fun and fast shape to rotary cut. You simply **rotate the ruler** between the two 60° lines.

Add on seam allowance to the <u>FINISHED</u> size of an Equilateral Triangle:

Add 3/4" to the height

Example: Desired finished height: 2 1/4" equilateral triangle

Height of strip to cut: 3"
2 1/4" + 3/4" = 3"

NOTE: You need only know the unfinished height of an equilateral triangle in order to start cutting. The length will automatically be correct after rotary cutting the triangle.

STEP ONE: Place one of the 3" strips on the mat. Left handed quilters will use the 60° line starting from the lower left edge of the ruler. Right handed quilters will use the 60° line starting from the lower right edge of the ruler. While placing the ruler on the strip, make sure the 60° line lines up with the bottom of the strip. Rotary cut.

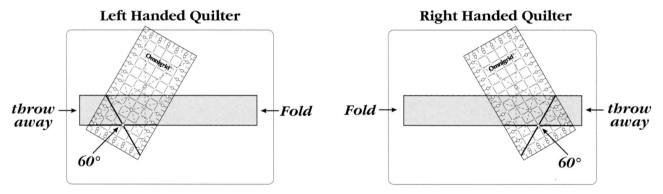

STEP TWO: **DO NOT ROTATE THE MAT.** Rotate the ruler so the opposite 60° line is now on the bottom of the strip. Carefully slide the ruler until it lines up with the sharp point of the original cut. Rotary cut. To make more triangles, just rotate the ruler between the appropriate 60° lines until you have the desired number of triangles.

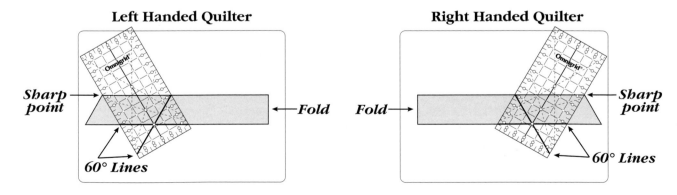

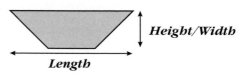

A full trapezoid is actually a rectangle with both ends cut off at an angle. Both angles can be the same, or they can be different angles. Trapezoids used in quiltmaking <u>usually have ends that are both cut at 45°</u>.

Add on seam allowance to the <u>FINISHED</u> size of a Full Trapezoid cut at 45°:

> **Add ¹/₂" to the height/width** (The words height and width are interchangeable)
> **Add 1 ¹/₄" to the length**

Example: Desired finished size: 2 ¹/₂" x 9" full trapezoid

Size of rectangle to cut: 3" x 10 ¹/₄"
2 ¹/₂" + ¹/₂" = 3"
9" + 1 ¹/₄" = 10 ¹/₄"

STEP ONE: Place one of the 3" strips on the mat. Cut a rectangle 3" x 10 ¹/₄". Left handed quilters position the ruler so the 45° mark on its lower left edge lines up with the left bottom of the rectangle. Right handed quilters position the ruler so the 45° mark on its lower right edge lines up with the right bottom of the rectangle. Carefully slide the ruler so you will be starting the cut **exactly** at the **lower** (left) right corner of the rectangle. If you start the cut left or right of the exact corner, your trapezoid will not be the correct size. Rotary cut.

Left Handed Quilter

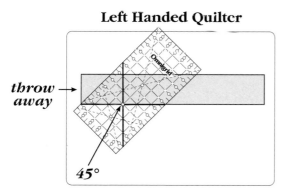

Right Handed Quilter

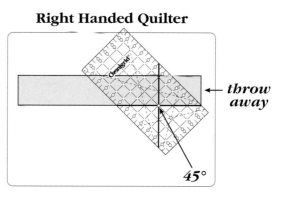

STEP TWO: Turn the mat 180°, half a turn. Left handed quilters, position the ruler so the opposite 45° mark on the upper left edge lines up with the bottom of the rectangle. Right handed quilters use the 45° mark on the upper right edge. Carefully slide the ruler so you will be finishing the cut exactly at the **upper** (left) right corner of the rectangle. Rotary cut.

Left Handed Quilter

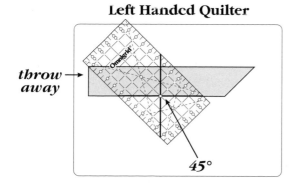

Right Handed Quilter

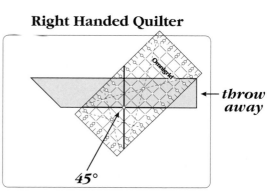

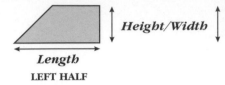

Height/Width

Length
LEFT HALF

Length
RIGHT HALF

𝒴our pattern will determine whether you need a left or right half trapezoid. Half trapezoids used in quiltmaking <u>have one end that is usually cut at a 45° angle.</u> The most famous pattern that uses left and right half trapezoids is the Attic Window.

Add on seam allowance to the <u>FINISHED</u> size of a Left or Right Half Trapezoid cut at 45°:

Add 1/2" to the height/width (The words height and width are interchangeable)
Add 7/8" to the length

Example: Desired finished size of a LEFT or RIGHT half trapezoid:
2 1/2" height x 6" length

Size of rectangle to cut: 3" x 6 7/8"
2 1/2" + 1/2" = 3"
6" + 7/8" = 6 7/8"

STEP ONE: Place one of the 3" strips on the mat. Cut one rectangle 3" x 6 7/8".

STEP TWO: The following diagrams show the left or right handed quilter how to cut a right and left half trapezoid. Position the ruler so the 45° mark on the lower (left) right edge lines up with the (left) right bottom of the rectangle. Carefully slide the ruler so you will be starting the cut exactly at the **lower** (left) right corner of the rectangle. Rotary cut.

Left Handed Quilter
Left Half Trapezoid
Right Side of Fabric Facing You

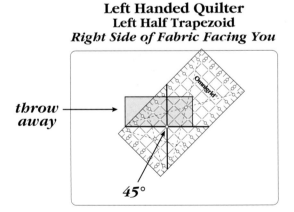

Right Handed Quilter
Left Half Trapezoid
Wrong Side of Fabric Facing You

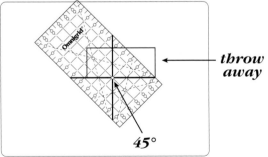

Left Handed Quilter
Right Half Trapezoid
Wrong Side of Fabric Facing You

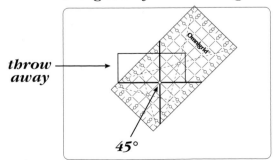

Right Handed Quilter
Right Half Trapezoid
Right Side of Fabric Facing You

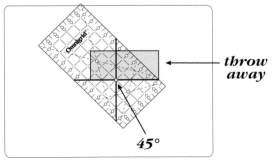

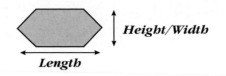

Height/Width

Length

You will see how valuable the angles are on the **Omnigrid®** ruler once you cut a single or double prism. In quiltmaking a double prism is a rectangle with both ends usually cut off at 45° angles.

Add on seam allowance to the <u>FINISHED</u> size of a Double Prism cut at 45°:

Add 1/2" to the height/width (The words height and width are interchangeable)

Add 3/4" to the length

Example: Desired finished size: 4 1/2" x 7 3/4" double prism

Size of rectangle to cut: 5" x 8 1/2"
4 1/2" + 1/2" = 5"
7 3/4" + 3/4" = 8 1/2"

STEP ONE: Place the 5" strip on the mat. Cut a rectangle 5" x 8 1/2". Now divide the unfinished width of the rectangle in half: 5" ÷ 2 = 2 1/2". With the ruler, measure in from the side of the rectangle 2 1/2" and place a small pencil mark on the top and bottom of the rectangle. This is the middle of the rectangle.

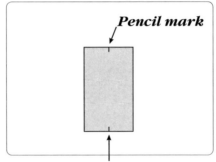

Pencil mark

Middle of the Rectangle

STEP TWO: Left handed quilters position the ruler diagonally on the rectangle so the 45° mark on its upper left edge lines up with the pencil mark. Right handed quilters position the ruler diagonally on the rectangle so the 45° mark on its upper right edge lines up with the pencil mark. Rotary cut.

Left Handed Quilter

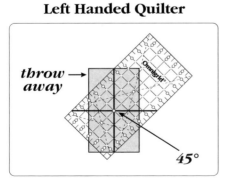

throw away

45°

Right Handed Quilter

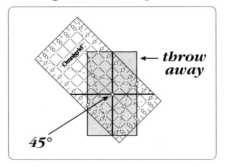

throw away

45°

Continued

STEP THREE: Left handed quilters rotate the mat counterclockwise 90°, one quarter of a turn. Right handed quilters rotate the mat clockwise 90°, one quarter of a turn. Now place the ruler so the opposite 45° marking runs through the pencil mark. Rotary cut.

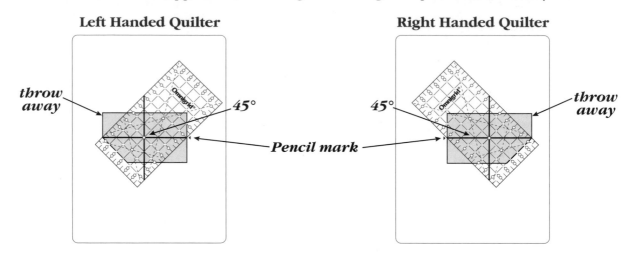

Left Handed Quilter   **Right Handed Quilter**

throw away   45°   45°   *throw away*

Pencil mark

STEP FOUR: To finish cutting the other end, simply repeat Steps Two and Three on the other half of the rectangle.

CUTTING A SINGLE PRISM

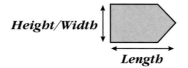

Height/Width

Length

$\mathcal{A}$ single prism is a rectangle with only one end usually cut off at 45° angles.

Add on seam allowance to the <u>FINISHED</u> size of a Single Prism cut at 45°:

> **Add 1/2" to the height/width** (The words height and width are interchangeable)

> **Add 5/8" to the length**

To cut a single prism, follow Steps One, Two and Three as described for cutting a Double Prism.

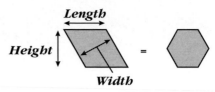

$\mathcal{E}$ven though this six-sided shape is called a hexagon, most of you will recognize it as the Grandma's Flower Garden shape. I found I could rotary cut a hexagon without templates from a **60° diamond**.

Add on seam allowance to the FINISHED size of a Hexagon:

> **Add ¹/2" to the height**
> **Add ¹/2" to the width**

Example: Desired finished size: 4 ¹/2" hexagon

Height of strip to cut: 5"
     4 ¹/2" + ¹/2" = 5"

STEP ONE: Place the 5" strip on the mat. Following Steps One and Two on page 29, cut a **5" - 60° diamond**. Place the diamond on the mat so the short points are facing the top and bottom of the mat.

STEP TWO: For this step, you must always divide the unfinished height of the 60° diamond in half. In this example: 5" ÷ 2 = 2 ¹/2". Position the ruler so the 2 ¹/2" marking runs through the two short points. For added accuracy, the upper 60° line should be on the lower left facet of the diamond for left handed quilters, and the upper 60° line should be on the lower right facet for right handed quilters. Rotary cut.

Left Handed Quilter	**Right Handed Quilter**
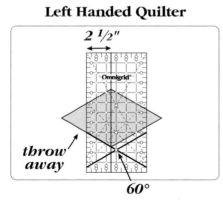	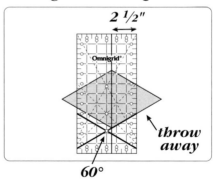

STEP THREE: Now rotate the mat 180°, half a turn, and position the ruler so the 2 ¹/2" marking again runs through the two short points. For added accuracy make sure the upper 60° line is on the (left) right bottom of the hexagon. Rotary cut.

Left Handed Quilter	**Right Handed Quilter**
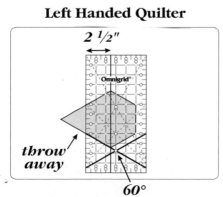	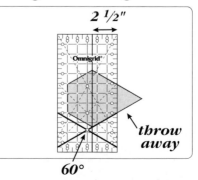

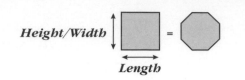

Height/Width $\updownarrow$ ☐ = ⬡

Length

*A*n octagon is an eight-sided shape. I didn't think there was a method for cutting this shape without the use of a template and scissors. I was wrong. After working with the **Omnigrid®** ruler, I discovered an easy method for cutting octagons. An octagon is a square with the four corners cut off.

Add on seam allowance to the <u>FINISHED</u> size of an Octagon:

> **Add 1/2" to the height/width** (The words height and width
>> are interchangeable)
> **Add 1/2" to the length**

Example: Desired finished size: 4 1/2" octagon

Size of square to cut: 5"
4 1/2" + 1/2" = 5"

STEP ONE: Place the 5" strip on the mat. Cut a 5" square. Place it diagonally on the mat so the **wrong** side is facing you for the next four cutting steps. With a pencil, lightly draw a diagonal line from corner to corner across the square, twice.

STEP TWO: For this step, you must always divide the size of the unfinished square in half. In this example: 5" ÷ 2 = 2 1/2". Position the ruler so the 2 1/2" line is on top of the vertical pencil line. Rotary cut.

Left Handed Quilter   **Right Handed Quilter**

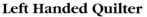
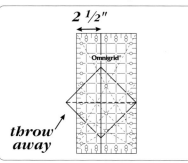

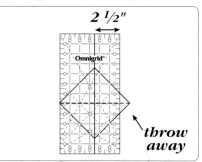

STEP THREE: Turn the mat 180°, half a turn, and position the ruler so the 2 1/2" line again covers the same vertical pencil line. Rotary cut.

Left Handed Quilter   **Right Handed Quilter**

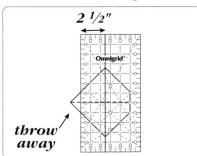
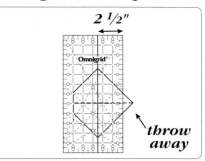

STEP FOUR: Turn the mat 90°, one quarter of a turn. Position the ruler so the 2 ½" line runs over the second vertical pencil line. Rotary cut.

Left Handed Quilter

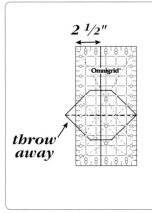

Right Handed Quilter

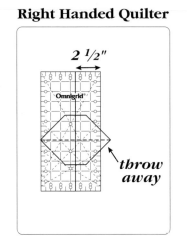

STEP FIVE: Turn the mat 180°, half a turn. Position the ruler so the 2 ½" line runs over the second vertical pencil line. Rotary cut.

Left Handed Quilter

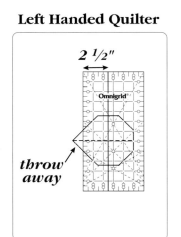

Right Handed Quilter

Height/Width = = *Long Sides* *Length*

I discovered this shape when I was drafting a Feathered Star pattern. It looked rather odd and I didn't know if I would be able to rotary cut it without templates. I did cut around a template the first few times. But the more I studied the kite shape, the more I realized it was a square cut in half to make two half square triangles, with one tip of each triangle cut off. I also came to understand that the two short sides have to be equal in length. The two long sides must also be equal in length. Once I gained this knowledge, cutting the kite shape was a breeze!

Add on seam allowance to the <u>FINISHED</u> size of a Square that will be cut into a Kite:

Add 7/8" to the height/width of a square (The words height and width are interchangeable)
Add 7/8" to the length of a square

Example: Desired finished length of the long side: 4 1/8"

Size of square to cut: 5"
4 1/8" + 7/8" = 5"

STEP ONE: Place the 5" strip on the mat. Cut a 5" square. Cut the square in half diagonally. Position the triangle so the long bias edge faces the top of the mat.

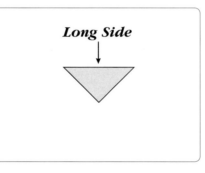

Long Side

STEP TWO: Now align the top of the ruler with the top of the triangle, and the tip of the triangle at the 5" marking - the unfinished size of the square. Rotary cut.

Left Handed Quilter

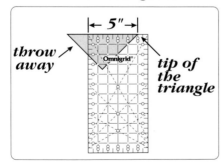

throw away |← 5" →| *tip of the triangle*

Right Handed Quilter

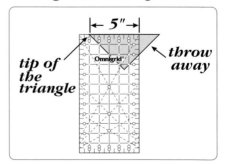

|← 5" →| *tip of the triangle*   *throw away*

NOTE: *Remember in Step Two, you will always use the size of the unfinished square as the measurement for recutting the triangle. For example: a 2" square, cut in half diagonally. In Step Two you will place the top of the ruler so it aligns with the top of the triangle, and the tip of the triangle is at the 2" line, the size of the unfinished square.*

$\mathcal{E}$arly on, I had never thought about cutting this shape without a template. I didn't think it could be done. The clipped square is used in several patterns, including the Bow Tie pattern. I challenged myself to work out a simple method to rotary cut a clipped square.

STEP ONE: You must first draw your desired pattern on graph paper to determine how much of the square you want clipped off. The line drawn on the graph paper for the clip will be called the stitching line.

STEP TWO: Add 1/4" seam allowance to the right of the stitching line. This is the cutting line.

STEP THREE: Draw a diagonal line from corner to corner on the drawn square.

Steps Two and Three

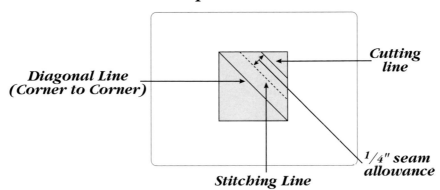

STEP FOUR: To determine the **correct** amount to be cut off, measure from the diagonal line to the cutting line.

FOR EXAMPLE: Suppose after drafting a 5" square, you determined the correct measurement from the diagonal line to the cutting line is 1 1/2". You would cut a 5" square and place it diagonally on the mat. Next position the ruler so the **correct** measurement, in this example, the 1 1/2" marking, runs through the opposite corners. Rotary cut.

Example

Left Handed Quilter   **Right Handed Quilter**

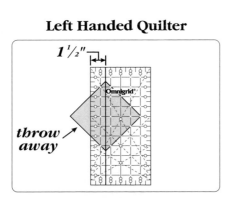

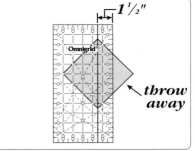

𝒟espite your careful attention when cutting, sewing and pressing, there are times when the quilt block is **slightly** out of square. For miniature work, I usually use a 6" square (with the 3" grid) ruler. For larger blocks I will use either the 9 ¹/₂", 12 ¹/₂" or 15" square ruler.

I want to show you two different methods of "squaring up" a **12 ¹/₂" unfinished** Lemoyne Star block. Either method may be used to "square up" virtually any block.

METHOD #1   (Using a 15" square **Omnigrid**® ruler)

STEP ONE: Divide the unfinished block size (12 ¹/₂") in half - 12 ¹/₂" ÷ 2 = 6 ¹/₄". Locate the 6 ¹/₄" marking on the top and to the right edge of the square ruler. You will notice the 6 ¹/₄" marking from the top intersects with the 6 ¹/₄" marking from the right side.

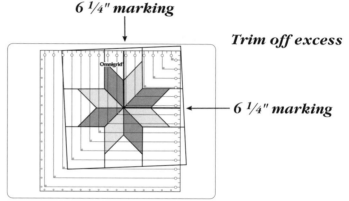

6 ¹/₄" marking

Trim off excess

6 ¹/₄" marking

STEP TWO: Place the 6 ¹/₄" intersection at the center of the 12 ¹/₂" star block. Trim any excess fabric that's beyond the top and right edge of the ruler. Rotate the mat 180°, half a turn, and repeat Step Two.

METHOD #2   (Using a 15" square **Omnigrid**® ruler)

STEP ONE: Turn the ruler 180°, half a turn. You will see yellow lines that run along the bottom, turn the corner, and run down the right side of the ruler. These solid yellow lines are spaced every ¹/₄".

STEP TWO: Place the ruler on top of the 12 ¹/₂" block so the star points on the top and right side of the block are touching the first ¹/₄" yellow line. Remember, the bottom of the ruler will be at the top of the block. Trim any excess fabric that's beyond the top and right edge of the ruler. Rotate the mat 180° and repeat Step Two. You now have a perfect ¹/₄" seam allowance around the whole block.

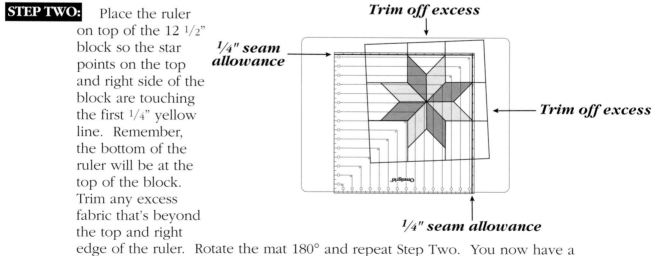

Trim off excess

¹/₄" seam allowance

Trim off excess

¹/₄" seam allowance

NOTE: *Be very careful when trimming. Always be sure you leave a ¹/₄" seam allowance around the whole block.*

Amish Melon Patch by Laurie Mace, 35" x 47". Notice how Laurie worked in different shades of solid colors, giving the quilt a very exciting look!

Dancing To A Different Tune by Laurie Mace, 26" x 37". Laurie wondered what would happen if she made mirror images of the G piece in the *Star At An Angle* pattern. This wallhanging is the result. Notice how neighboring stars are tipped left-right.

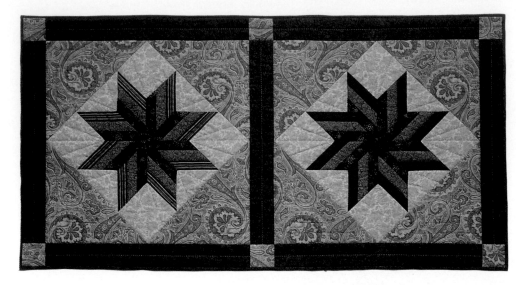

Spinning Star On Point by the author, 25" x 48". Quilted by Debbie Grow. I use this wallhanging as a sample to show students how powerful color and fabric scale are. The two stars are identical except for one of the fabrics!

Feathered Star On Point by the author, 36" square. Quilted by Debbie Grow. The Feathered Star is one of my favorite patterns. Notice how the border makes the star appear as if it has exploded.

Lone Star by Marcia Rickansrud, 23" square. Marcia chose to border her small Lone Star with squares and nine patch cornerstones.

Square Within A Star by Marcia Rickansrud, 33" square. If you love plaids and stripes this quilt is for you. What a wonderful piece!

Feathered Star by Debbie Grow, 29" square. Debbie is a master of appliqué, and I think you can see why! She used an appliqué pattern from Jeana Kimball's book, **Fairmeadow**, to embellish her Feathered Star.

Melon Patch by the author, 35" x 46". Notice how the dark half square triangles appear to be the eight points of a star around the center octagon!

Star In The Window by the author, 28" x 38".

The concept of a "Master Pattern" came about after I made twelve Variable Stars and began to wonder about the effect of different settings and borders.

Although the backgrounds are the same and the stars are made from the same color family, notice how differently the wallhangings look when finished.

Star At An Angle by the author, 27" x 38".

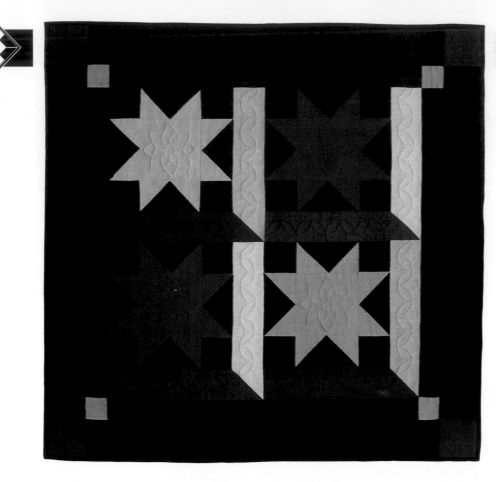

Amish Star In The Window by Laurie Mace, 27" square. Laurie decided to use different shades of solids for each star. Some stars recede into the background and some don't.

Spinning Star by Laurie Mace, 21" square. A very challenging color exercise for Laurie. She used varying shades of purple for the star. The border is pieced with parallelograms.

Photos on Page 41, 45, 46
Block Size: 8" finished square
Seam allowance: 1/4"

Shapes Used In This "Master" Pattern and How To Cut Them:

Shape **A, D** - Square - Page 17
Shape **B** - Half Square Triangle
    Method #1 - Page 18
    Method # 2 - Page 19
Shape **C** - Quarter Square Triangle
    Method #1 - Page 21
    Method # 2 - Page 22

Cutting Procedure:

(For One Block)
A - Cut 1 - 4 1/2" square, dark.

B - *Method #1* - Cut 4 - 2 7/8" squares,
dark. Cut in half diagonally, once.

Method #2 - Cut 1 - 2 1/2" x 13" strip, dark.
Use the #96 Half Square Ruler.
Place the 2" marking on the bottom or
top of the strip. You need eight triangles.

C - *Method # 1* - Cut 1 - 5 1/4" square,
light. Cut in half diagonally, twice.

Method #2 - Cut 1 - 2 5/8" x 14" strip, light.
Use the # 98 Quarter Square Ruler. Place the
4" marking on the bottom or top of the strip.
You need four triangles.

D - Cut 4 - 2 1/2" squares, light.

Sewing Procedure:

1. Sew one **B** to **C**. Press to **B**. Add another **B** to
the other side of **C**. Press to **B**. Cut off dog
ears. Make four sets.

2. Sew one **D** to the **BC** set. Add another **D** to
the other side of the **BC** set. Press to **D**. Make
two sets.

3. Sew a **BC** set to one side of **A**. Add
another **BC** set to the other side of **A**.
Press to **A**.

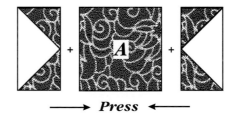

4. Butt, pin and sew into rows according
to the diagram. Press to **Row 1**.

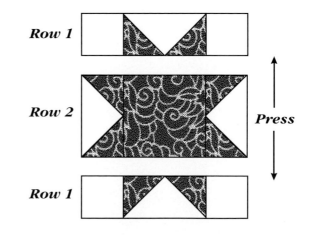

Photos on Page 45, 46
Block Size: 10" square finished
Seam Allowance: 1/4"

*Shapes Used In Addition To The "Master"
Pattern and How To Cut Them:*

Shape **E** - Right Half Trapezoid - Page 32
Shape **F** - Left Half Trapezoid - Page 32

Cutting Procedure:

Follow the cutting and sewing procedure to make a Variable Star block.

E - Cut 1 - 2 1/2" x 10 7/8" rectangle, dark. Cut into a right half trapezoid. (Left handed quilters cut with the wrong side of the fabric facing you. Right handed quilters cut with the right side of the fabric facing you).

F - Cut 1 - 2 1/2" x 10 7/8" rectangle, light. Cut into a left half trapezoid. (Left handed quilters cut with the right side of the fabric facing you. Right handed quilters cut with the wrong side of the fabric facing you).

Sewing Procedure:

1. Pin **F** to **E** right sides together. With the wrong side of **F** facing you, start sewing and stop sewing 1/4" from the edge and back tack. Do not press yet.

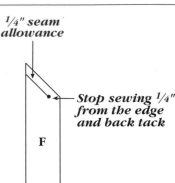

1/4" seam allowance

→ *Stop sewing 1/4" from the edge and back tack*

F

2. Sewing the Star to the Attic Window - With the wrong side of the light **F** piece facing you, pin to the correct side of the star. Start sewing from the top of the **F** piece. Stop sewing 1/16th of an inch from the **EF** seam line and back tack.

   Cut the thread and remove from the machine. Now with the wrong side of the star facing you, pin and sew to the **E** piece. Stop sewing 1/16th of an inch from the **EF** seam line and back tack. Press seams towards the **E** and **F** pieces.

3. Make six Star In the Window blocks and set together. If desired, add borders.

STAR AT AN ANGLE

Photos on Page 41, 45
Block Size: 9 3/4" square finished
Seam Allowance: 1/4"

Shapes Used In Addition To The "Master" Pattern and How To Cut Them:

Shape **G** - Half of an Untrue Rectangle - Page 24

Cutting Procedure:

Follow the cutting and sewing procedure to make a Variable Star block.

G - Cut 2 - 2 ½" x 10 ¾" rectangles, medium dark. Cut in half diagonally. Left handed quilters cut with the wrong side of the fabric facing you. Right handed quilters cut with the right side of the fabric facing you. (These pieces are slightly larger than needed. You will square up the block later).

Sewing Procedure:

1. Sewing the Half Rectangles to the Star: With the wrong side of the star facing you, offset the long bias edge of **G** by ⅛". The long thin part of **G** will hang over the star by 2 ¼". Sew to the star. Press to **G**. Trim off the odd looking dog ears. After cutting off the dog ears, the **G** piece will be offset from the corner ⅜" at one end and ⅛" at the other end. See the diagram. Sew another **G** on the opposite side. Press to **G**. Trim dog ears.

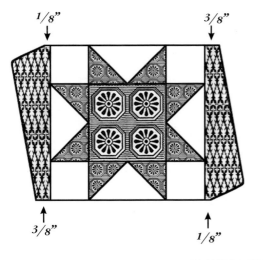

2. Sew the remaining two **G** pieces on. Again have the large edge of **G** hang over ⅛" when starting to sew. Press to **G** and trim all dog ears.

3. Square up the block to 10 ¼". Make sure you leave a ¼" seam allowance around the whole block.

4. Make six stars and set together. If desired, add borders.

Photo on Page 43
Block Size: 8" finished square
Seam Allowance: ¼"

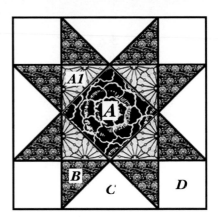

Shapes Used In Addition To The "Master" Pattern and How To Cut Them:

Shape **A** - Square - Page 17
Shape **A1** - Half Square Triangle
  Method #1 - Page 18
  Method #2 - Page 19
Shape **B, C, D** - Follow the cutting procedure from the "Master" pattern.

Cutting Procedure:

A - Cut 1 - 3 ⁵⁄₁₆" square, medium light or medium dark. (3 ⁵⁄₁₆" is located between 3 ¼" and 3 ⅜").

A1 - *Method #1* - Cut 2 - 2 ⅞" squares, contrasting medium light or medium dark. Cut in half diagonally, once.

Method #2 - Cut 1 - 2 ½" x 7" strip, contrasting medium light or medium dark. Use the #96 Half Square Ruler. Place the 2" marking on the bottom or top of the strip. You need four triangles.

Sewing Procedure:

1. Sew two **A1**s to the opposite sides of **A**. Press to **A**. Add **A1** to the other two sides. Press to **A**.

Continue sewing the block together as shown in Steps 1 and 2 on page 47. For Step 3, insert the **A/A1** unit instead of the **A** square. Continue on to Step 4.

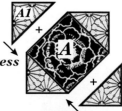

Make as many stars as desired and set together. Add borders.

Photos on Page 41, 44

Block Size: 6" finished Melon Patch

Seam allowance: 1/4"

Shapes Used In This Pattern and How To Cut Them:

Shape **A** - Octagon - Page 36

Shape **B** - Half Square Triangle
   Method #1 - Page 18

Shape **C** - Quarter Square Triangle
   Method #1 - Page 21
   Method # 2 - Page 22

Cutting Procedure for the Melon Patch:

A - MEDIUM DARK - Cut 9 - 6 1/2" squares.
   Using the 3 1/4" marking on the ruler, recut into nine octagons.

A - LIGHT - Cut 4 - 6 1/2" squares. Using the 3 1/4" marking on the ruler, recut into four octagons.

B - MEDIUM DARK - *Method #1* - Cut 1 - 2 3/4" x 24" strip. Cut into eight 2 3/4" squares. Recut in half diagonally.

B - LIGHT - *Method #1* - Cut 1 - 2 3/4" x 40" strip. Cut into fourteen 2 3/4" squares. Recut in half diagonally.

C - *Method #1* - Cut 2 - 7 1/4" squares, light. Cut in half diagonally, twice.

   Method #2 - Cut 1 - 3 5/8" x 44" strip, light. Use the #98 Quarter Square Ruler. Place the 6" marking on the bottom or top of the strip. You need eight triangles.

Sewing Procedure:

1. **Unit 1:** Sew one light **B** to the proper corners of the medium dark **A**. Press to **A**. Make one set. If necessary, square up the block. The block will measure 6 1/2" square.

→ *Press* ←

2. **Unit 2:** Sew one light **B** to the proper corners of medium dark **A**. Press to **A**. Make four sets. If necessary, square up the block so the sewn **A/B** sides equal 6 1/2".

→ *Press* ←

3. **Unit 3:** Sew one light **B** to the proper corners of medium dark **A**. Press to **A**. Make four sets. If necessary, square up the block so the sewn **A/B** sides equal 6 1/2".

→ *Press* ←

4. **Unit 4:** Sew one medium dark **B** to the proper corners of light **A**. Press to **B**. Make four sets. Cut off dog ears. If necessary, square up the block. The block will measure 6 1/2" square.

← *Press* →

5. Following the diagram, butt, pin and sew the Melon Patches into rows. Press the seams towards the medium dark Melon Patches. Sew **B** light triangles to each corner.

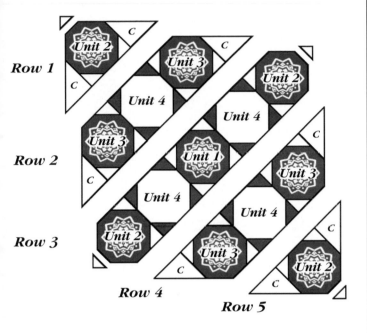

6. Sew the rows together. It doesn't matter which way you press these seams. Cut off dog ears. The wallhanging will now measure 23 ¼" square.

Inner Border

7. Cut 2 - 2" x 23 ¼" strips, dark. Sew to the top and bottom of the wallhanging. Press outward.

   Cut 2 - 2" x 26 ¼" strips, dark. Sew to the sides of the wallhanging. Press outward.

CHECKERED BORDER

Cutting Procedure:

Cut 2 - 2 ½" x 38" strips, dark.

Cut 1 - 2 ½" x 38" strip, light.

Sewing Procedure:

8. Sew one dark strip to the light. Press to the dark. Sew the other dark strip to the light strip. Press to the dark. Cut the sewn strips into fourteen 2 ½" sections.

Press

9. Cut 1 - 2 ½" x 33" strip, medium dark. Cut 2 - 2 ½" x 33" strips, light.

   Sew one light strip to the medium dark strip. Press to the medium dark strip. Sew the other light strip to the medium dark strip. Press to the medium dark strip. Cut the sewn strips into twelve 2 ½" sections.

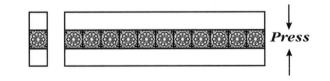

Press

10. Following the diagram, butt, pin and sew the checkered border together. It doesn't matter which way you press the seams. Make two sets. Sew the checkered border to the top and bottom of the wallhanging. Press seams towards the inner border.

Top and Bottom Border: Cut 2 - 6" x the top and bottom measurement of the wallhanging, light.

Cut 4 - 6" squares, medium dark.

Sew one 6" square to the ends of the top and bottom border. Press to the light. Sew this border on after sewing on the side borders.

Side Border: Cut 2 - 6" x the measurement of the wallhanging. Sew to the sides of the wallhanging. Press outward. Add top and bottom borders.

NOTE: You could very easily make a quilt by only using the Checkered Border pattern.

Photos on Page 42, 46
Block Size: 14 ½" square finished
Seam allowance: ¼"

Shapes Used In This "Master" Pattern and How To Cut Them:

Shape **A, B, C** - 45° Diamonds - Page 26
Shape **D** - Quarter Square Triangle
    Method #1 - Page 21
    Method # 2 - Page 22
Shape **E** - Square - Page 17

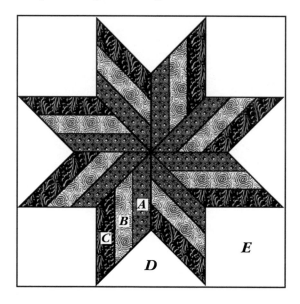

Cutting Procedure:

A - Cut 1 - 1 ½" x 44" strip, medium dark.

B - Cut 1 - 1 ½" x 44" strip, medium light.

C - Cut 1 - 1 ½" x 44" strip, dark.

D - *Method #1* - Cut 1 - 7 ¼" square, light. Cut in half diagonally, twice.

    Method #2 - Cut 1 - 3 ⅝" x 19" strip, light. Use the # 98 Quarter Square Ruler. Place the 6" marking on the bottom or top of the strip. You need four triangles.

E - Cut 4 - 4 ¾" squares, light.

Sewing Procedure:

1. Pin the strips together according to the diagram shown in #2. The strips are staggered 1 ½" in to allow for maximum use of fabric. Sew **A** strip to **B** strip . Press to **B**. Sew **C** strip to **B** strip. Press to **C**. The three sewn strips will now measure 3 ½" in height.

2. Cut eight 3 ½" diagonal strips. When you are cutting the 3 ½" diagonal strips, make sure the 45° marking runs along the bottom of the strip and the ruler is 3 ½" in from the cut edge.

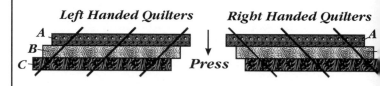

NOTE: *After cutting two 3 ½" diagonal cuts, cut a new 45° angle on the remaining strip. If you don't, you will start to work out of square with the 45° angle.*

3. Sewing the diamonds into pairs - Take two of the diamonds and pin together. Start sewing and stop ¼" from the bottom edge and back tack. Press according to the diagram. Cut off dog ears. Make four sets.

4. Sew two sets together to make a half. Remember to stop 1/4" from the bottom edge and back tack. Press according to the diagram. Repeat again for the other half of the star.

Stop sewing 1/4" and back tack

← **Press**

5. Pin the two halves together. Start sewing 1/4" in from the diamond edge, back tack, continue scwing and stop 1/4" from the end of the last diamond edge. Back tack. It doesn't matter which way you press the center seam.

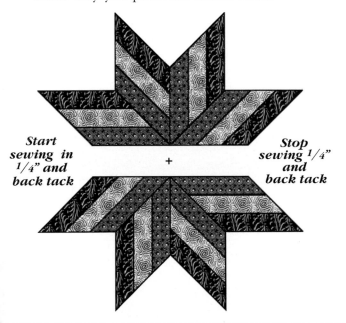

Start sewing in 1/4" and back tack

Stop sewing 1/4" and back tack

6. Sewing the **D** Triangle to the Star - With the wrong side of the diamond facing you, pin to the correct side of the **D** triangle. Start sewing from the outside tip of the diamond. Stop sewing 1/16th of an inch from the inside diamond seam line and back tack.

   Cut the thread and remove from the machine. Now with the wrong side of the **D** triangle facing you, pin and sew to the diamond. Stop

sewing 1/16th of an inch from the inside diamond seam line and back tack. Press to **D**. Do all four sides this way. Cut off all dog ears.

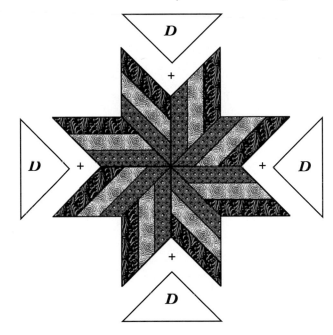

7. Sewing the **E** Square to the Star - With the wrong side of the diamond facing you, pin to the correct side of the **E** square. Stop scwing 1/16th of an inch from the inside diamond seam line and back tack. Cut the thread and remove from the machine.

   Now with the wrong side of the **E** square facing you, pin to the other diamond. Start sewing. Stop sewing 1/16th of an inch from the inside diamond seam line and back tack. Press to **E**. Do all four corners this way.

NOTE: *When setting in seams, always stop 1/16th of an inch from the inside diamond seams and back tack. By doing this, you will prevent a pleat from forming on the front of the star.*

SPINNING STAR ON POINT

Follow the cutting and sewing procedures to make a Spinning Star.

To Set On Point: Cut 2 - 11 1/2" squares of desired color. Cut in half diagonally. (These triangles are slightly oversized. You will "square up" later.)

Sew one large triangle to each side of the Spinning Star. Press toward the triangles. Cut off all dog ears. "Square up" the block. Add borders if desired.

Photo on Page 43

Block Size: Large Star 25 1/4" square finished
Block Size: Small Star 14 1/2" square finished
Seam allowance: 1/4"

Shapes Used In This Pattern and How To Cut Them:

Shape **A, B, C, D, E** - 45° Diamonds - Page 26
Shape **F** - Quarter Square Triangle
    Method #1 - Page 21
    Method #2 - Page 22
Shape **G** - Square - Page 17

NOTE: *The cutting measurements and sewing procedures for the small Lone Star are in parentheses.*

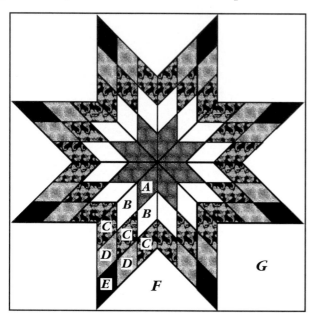

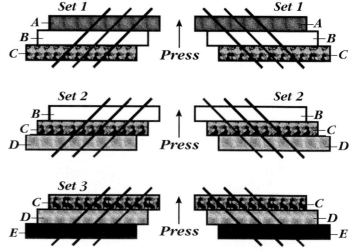

Cutting Procedure for Large and Small Lone Star:

A - Cut 1 - 2 1/4" x 44" strip, dark.
        (1 - 1 1/2" x 22" strip)

B - Cut 2 - 2 1/4" x 44" strips, light.
        (2 - 1 1/2" x 22" strips)

C - Cut 3 - 2 1/4" x 44" strips, contrasting dark.
        (3 - 1 1/2" x 22" strips)

D - Cut 2 - 2 1/4" x 44" strips, medium dark.
        (2 - 1 1/2" x 22" strips)

E - Cut 1 - 2 1/4" x 44" strip, contrasting medium dark. (1 - 1 1/2" x 22" strip)

F - *Method #1* - Cut 1 - 11 3/4" (7 1/4") square, light. Cut in half diagonally, twice.

    Method #2 - Cut 1 - 5 7/8" x 33" strip (3 5/8" x 19" strip), light. Use the #98L Quarter Square Ruler.   Place the 10 1/2" (6") marking on the bottom or top of the strip. You need four triangles.

G - Cut 4 - 7 7/8" (4 3/4") squares, light.

Sewing Procedure:

1. Pin and sew the strips together according to the diagram. The strips are staggered 1 1/2" (1") in to allow for maximum use of fabric. Press according to the diagram. Each set of three sewn strips will now measure 5 3/4" (3 1/2") in height.

    Cut eight 2 1/4" (1 1/2") diagonal strips. When you are cutting the diagonal strips, make sure the 45° marking runs along the bottom of the strip and the ruler is 2 1/4" (1 1/2") in from the cut edge.

NOTE: *After cutting two 2 1/4" (1 1/2") diagonal cuts, cut a new 45° angle on the remaining strip. If you don't, you will start to work out of square with the 45° angle.*

2. Pin (the diagonal strips will be offset by ¹/₄")
   and sew the recut diagonal strips together to
   form eight large diamonds. Press in the
   direction of the arrow. Cut off dog ears.

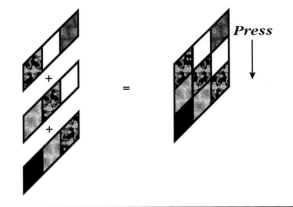

Press

3. Sewing the Diamonds into Pairs - Butt and pin
   two of the diamonds together. Start sewing and
   stop ¹/₄" from the bottom edge and back tack.
   Press according to the diagram. Cut off dog
   ears. Make four sets.

*Stop
sewing ¹/₄"
and back tack*

← *Press*

4. Butt, pin and sew two sets together to make a
   half. Remember to stop ¹/₄" from the bottom
   edge and back tack. Press according to the
   diagram. Repeat again for the other half of
   the star.

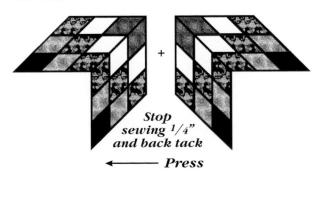

*Stop
sewing ¹/₄"
and back tack*

← *Press*

5. Butt and pin the two halves together. Start
   sewing ¹/₄" in from the diamond edge, back
   tack, continue sewing and stop ¹/₄" from the
   end of the last diamond edge. Back tack. It
   doesn't matter which way you press the center
   seam.

*Start
sewing in
¹/₄" and
back tack*   +   *Stop
sewing ¹/₄"
and back
tack*

6. Sewing the **F** Triangle to the Star - With the
   wrong side of the diamond facing you, pin to
   the correct side of the **F** triangle. Start sewing
   from the outside tip of the diamond. Stop
   sewing ¹/16th of an inch from the inside
   diamond seam line and back tack.

Continued

Cut the thread and remove from the machine. Now with the wrong side of the **F** triangle facing you, pin and sew to the diamond. Stop sewing 1/16th of an inch from the inside diamond seam line and back tack. Press to **F**. Do all four sides this way. Cut off all dog ears.

7. Sewing the **G** Square to the Star - With the wrong side of the diamond facing you, pin to the correct side of the **G** square. Stop sewing 1/16th of an inch from the inside diamond seam line and back tack. Cut the thread and remove from the machine.

Now with the wrong side of the **G** square facing you, pin to the other diamond. Start sewing. Stop sewing 1/16th of an inch from the inside diamond seam line and back tack. Press to **G**. Do all four corners this way.

NOTE: *When setting in seams, always stop 1/16th of an inch from the inside diamond seams and back tack. By doing this, you will prevent a pleat from forming on the front of the star.*

Photos on Page 42, 44
Block Size: 20 7/8" finished square
Seam allowance: 1/4"

Shapes Used In This "Master" Pattern and How To Cut Them:

Shape **A, A1, F** - Half Square Triangle
 Method #1 - Page 18
Shape **B, H** - Square - Page 17
Shape **C** - 45° Diamond - Page 26
Shape **D** - Kite - Page 38
Shape **E, I** Quarter Square Triangle
 Method #1 - Page 21
Shape **G** - Octagon - Page 36

Cutting Procedure:

A - DARK - Cut 2 - 2" x 25" strips.

A - LIGHT - Cut 2 - 2" x 25" strips.
 Position one light strip on top of the dark strip, right sides together. Cut into twenty four 2" squares. Recut in half diagonally to make forty eight triangles of each color.

A1 - Cut 1 - 2" x 17" strip, light. Cut into eight 2" squares. Recut in half diagonally for sixteen triangles.

B - Cut 1 - 1 5/8" x 14" strip, dark. Cut into eight 1 5/8" squares.

C - Cut 1 - 1 5/8" x 23" strip, dark. Using the 45° marking on the ruler, recut into eight 1 5/8" 45° diamonds.

D - Cut 4 - 5 3/8" squares, medium dark. Cut in half diagonally. Using the 5 3/8" marking on the ruler, recut into eight kite shapes.

E - *Method #1* - Cut 1 - 3 7/8" square, light. Cut in half diagonally, twice.

F - *Method #1* - Cut 2 - 2 3/4" squares light. Cut in half diagonally.

G - Cut 1 - 6 7/8" square, medium dark. Using the 3 7/16" marking on the ruler (3 7/16" is located between 3 3/8" and 3 1/2"), recut into an octagon.

H - Cut 4 - 6 5/8" squares, light.

I - *Method #1* - Cut 1 - 9 7/8" square, light. Cut in half diagonally twice.

Sewing Procedure:

1. Sew one light triangle to one dark triangle. Cut the dog ears off BEFORE carefully pressing to the dark. Make forty eight of these squares. The squares will now be 1 5/8".

UNIT 1
2. **STRIP 1** - Sew **A1** to the proper side of **C** diamond first. Press seam to **A1**. Cut off dog ears. Make four sets.

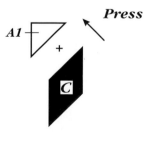

Continued

3. Add three squares and press seams as shown in the diagram. Make four strips.

STRIP 2

4. Sew **A1** to the proper side of **C** diamond first. Press seam to **A1**. Cut off dog ears. Make four sets.

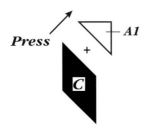

---

5. Add three squares and press seams as shown in the diagram. Sew **B** square on and press this seam towards **B**. Make four strips.

---

6. Pin and sew **Strip 1** to the **H** square. (Make sure the diamond point hangs 3/8" over the edge of the **H** square). Press to **H**. Do not cut off the diamond point.

Butt, pin and sew **Strip 2** to the **H** square. (Make sure the diamond point hangs 3/8" over the edge of **H**). Press to **H**. Do not cut off the diamond point. Make four units.

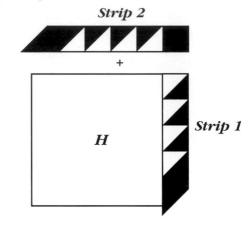

UNIT 2

7. **STRIP 1** - Sew three squares together as shown and add an **A1**. Press seams towards **A1**. Make four sets.

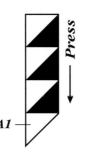

---

8. **STRIP 2** -   Sew three squares together as shown and add an **A1** on the bottom. Press seams towards **A1**. Add a **B** square to the top and press seam toward **B**. Make four sets.

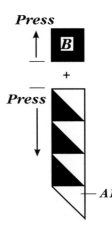

9. Sew **Strip 1** to the **I** triangle. **Stop** sewing where the dark dots are shown on the diagram. (This is called a partial seam. You will finish sewing this seam later). Press seam to **I** piece.

Butt, pin and sew **Strip 2** to the other side of the **I** piece. Again, **stop** sewing where the dark dots are shown on the diagram. Press to **I**.

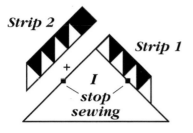

10. Sew **D** to **E**. Press to **D**. Make four sets.

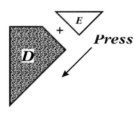

11. Following the diagram, sew **D** to **Unit 2**. Press to **D**. Butt, pin and sew the **DE** set on next. Press to **DE**. Cut off all dog ears. Make four units.

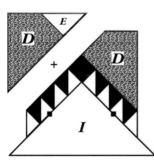

Unit 3
12. Sew an **F** triangle to four sides of the octagon. Press to **F**.

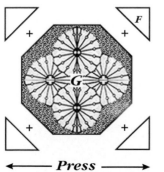

Assembling The Feathered Star Block:

Row 1
13. Following the diagram, sew a **Unit 1** to both sides of a **Unit 2**. Sew only between the two arrows. Fold the **I** piece out of the way as shown. (The partial seams will be sewn last). Press seams towards **Unit 2**. Make two sets.

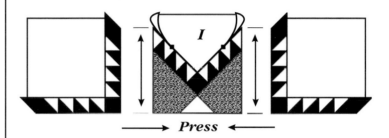

Row 2
14. Sew a **Unit 2** to both sides of **Unit 3**, the octagon section. Press seams away from the octagon section.

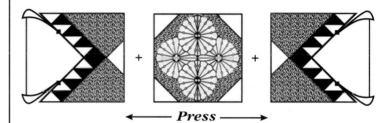

15. Butt, pin and sew **Row 1** to **Row 2**. Add the other **Row 1** to **Row 2**. Matching the **C** diamond tip with the **I** triangle tip, finish sewing the partial seams closed. By doing this, you will have a perfect 1/4" seam allowance around the whole block. Cut off dog ears. Add borders if desired.

FEATHERED STAR ON POINT

Follow the cutting and sewing procedures to make a Feathered Star.

To Set On Point: Cut 2 - 16" squares, of desired color. Cut in half diagonally. (These triangles are slightly oversized. You will "square up" later).

Sew one large triangle to each side of the Feathered Star. Press toward the triangles. Cut off all dog ears. "Square up" the block. Add borders if desired.

After working with **Omnigrid®** rulers for a few years, I have found them to be invaluable not only in quiltmaking, but in many other areas as well. The following is a list of **Omnigrid®** rulers and some particular uses:

1" x 6"

- Checking 1/4" seam allowance for quiltmaking
- 3/16" turn under seam allowance for appliqué
- 3/16" zipper installation
- Hem marking

4" x 4"

- Drafting in small detail
- Miniature quiltmaking
- Cutting and squaring blocks 4" and under

6" Square
(with 45° and 60° angles)

- Drafting in small detail
- Secondary cutting on smaller pieces
- Lap work
- Checking finished size of small blocks

6" Square
(with 3" grid in upper right hand corner)

- Checking diagonal half squares
- Miniatures
- Perfect for "squaring up" blocks

3" x 18"
and
3" x 18"
(Gridded)

- Secondary cutting of strips
- 45° and 60° angles
- Great for all around drafting
- 3" x 18" gridded ruler has 1/16" marking
- Great for Seminole work
- Cross Stitch
- Pattern grading

6" x 12"

- Portable and convenient for classes
- All secondary cutting
- 45° and 60° angles
- Cutting 1/4" fringe on Ultra Suede

6" x 24"

- A must for cutting long strips
- Cutting long borders
- Cutting bias strips
- Cutting all angles - 30°, 45°, 60°
- Cutting across strata (strips of fabric sewn together with 1/4" seam allowances)
- Excellent all around use by left and right handed people

9 1/2" Square
12 1/2" Square
15" Square

- Cutting squares up to 15"
- Checking triangles
- "Squaring Up" blocks
- Checking finished size
- Cutting borders larger than 6"
- Portable light table

❧ ❧ ❧ ❧ ❧

#96 *and* #96L Triangle

- #96 - Cut half square triangles up to 6"
- #96L - Cut half square triangles up to 8"
- 1/4" seam allowances are already designed into the markings on the ruler - no more guesswork or ruined blocks

❧ ❧ ❧ ❧ ❧

#98 *and* #98L Triangle

- #98 - Cut quarter square triangles up to 8" on the long side
- #98L - Cut quarter square triangles up to 12" on the long side
- 1/4" seam allowances are already designed into the markings on the ruler - no more guesswork or ruined blocks
- I call the #98 and #98L the "Great Fabric Saver" ruler. You cut strips of fabric, not squares. Consequently, you don't end up with an odd looking piece of fabric that has one or more squares cut out of it.

❧ ❧ ❧ ❧ ❧

Some other general uses for the Omnigrid® rulers:

Weaving

- Creating a draft of your pattern
- Charting your design
- Cutting strips for rag weaving
- Blocking
- Checking grain line

❧ ❧ ❧ ❧ ❧

Tailoring/Clothing

- Marking buttonholes
- Marking darts
- Marking zippers, tucks and pleats
- Hemming
- Cutting bias strips
- Cutting cuffs
- Cutting ribbing
- Cutting Ultra Suede

❧ ❧ ❧ ❧ ❧

Graphic Arts

- Mat cutting
- Framing
- Layout alignment

❧ ❧ ❧ ❧ ❧

Wall Papering

- Mitering corners
- Cutting straight edges
- Trimming for borders or top of paper

PROBLEM	HOW TO PREVENT	HOW TO FIX
ROTARY CUTTER		
• *Hand fatigue while cutting*	Refer to the rotary cutter section on pages 6-8 for tips on selecting and handling your cutter.	Try rotary cutting with the bottom of the cutter in the palm of your hand. Also position your first finger on the etched ridge located on the side of the cutter.
	The cutter may have a build-up of lint around the blade, thus preventing it from moving freely. Or the blade may be dull.	Clean the cutter frequently and put a small drop of sewing machine oil on the blade when assembling.
	Install a new blade frequently.	Replace dull blade.
• *Rotary cutter skips a thread while cutting*	Keep a sharp blade in the cutter. To prevent damage to the blade, keep the cutter closed when not in use. Examine cutter blade if you drop it. Do not cut over pins.	Blade has been nicked. The only way to fix is to replace the old blade.
• *Rotary cutter drags through the fabric*	Maintain proper blade tension.	Loosen or tighten the screw as appropriate.
	Always keep a sharp blade in your cutter. Change regularly.	Change the blade. It may be dull.
	Develop a "feel" for using uniform hand pressure on the cutter.	Apply more pressure.
	Don't try to cut too many layers of fabric.	Same as How To Prevent
	Always hold the cutter at a 45° angle to the ruler.	Increase or decrease angle to make it 45°.
• *Blades dull quickly*	Do not cut on wood, glass, plastic, etc.	Purchase a mat that is designed for rotary cutting.
• *Strips are not straight after cutting. A slight "V" is at the fold*	Always "resquare" the fabric with the fold every 6".	Don't try to use strips that are not absolutely straight. Cut new strips.
	Do not move the fabric from right to left during cutting. Rotate the mat 180°, half a turn, instead and then continue cutting.	Develop a habit of rotating the mat instead of rotating the fabric on the mat.